BEAT THE MARKET BY THE BEST LEADING STOCKS

How intelligent investors make money in Stocks with simple - transparent - quantitative strategies

Shin Nakamoto

Table of Contents

INTRODUCTION

The stock market is always a mystery. It is never clear, or coherent, or easy to understand for all of us. The science of business administration (BA, MBA), theories of fundamental analysis (FA), technical analysis (TA), many investing strategies have been derived for a long time. We cannot count the vast number of investing guidance books, finance websites, finance news, market newsletters, forums, discussion groups, consulting…; however, most of them only waste paper, time, and money of investors. Practically investors are swimming in the sea of information, but could not see the shore or the route to be successful. It is quite complicated for them to win the profits in this game.

Is this possible to get rich in the stock market?

That is a first-rate question to answer.

The answer is Yes, because the rich are still getting richer and richer in the stock market; they hold the shares of powerful enterprises which make their asset to increase day by day, associating with their stock's value.

The answer is Yes, because investment funds, investment management companies, the large investors still gain money from this market. If they do not, they will stop within some years.

The answer is Yes, because many stocks increase double, or triple every year, some examples:

1st half of year 2019: Shopify Inc. (SHOP): price rose from 122 to 336; The Trade Desk, Inc. (TTD): price rose from 110 to 278; Paycom

Software, Inc. (PAYC): price rose from 120 to 240; Everbridge, Inc. (EVBG): price rose from 45 to 102, ...

The year 2018: Amedisys, Inc. (AMED): price rose from 55 to 130; Sarepta Therapeutics, Inc. (SRPT): price rose from 55 to 150; Medifast, Inc. (MED): price rose from 70 to 250.

Moreover, there are many stocks that increase several dozen times or several hundred times in years, such as Microsoft Corporation (MSFT); Amazon.com, Inc. (AMZN); Apple Inc. (AAPL); Alphabet Inc. (GOOGL).

Another side, the answer is No, because the number of investors who lose money is enormous, chiefly the non-professional investors, the individual investors.

Why are many people NOT?

It is not easy to have a complete answer, but it is not difficult to have almost enough one, as below:

Knowledge and skills: Investors do not have specified knowledge, or not spend time to invest seriously, or invest spontaneously with non-quality advice from their friends, relatives, or brokers.

Instincts of humans prevent them from winning stock investing or trading: Hasty mentality, quickly making money expectation, impatience, gambling psychology, greed, fear, arrogance, and ego.

Applying some methods of investment mechanically without understanding or backtest enough: Fundamental analysis (FA) and technical analysis (TA) without verification, or in an extreme way.

Rubbish information: Too much information about finance, business, investment consultancy on the internet, books, newspapers cause the investors confused or lose their independence in analysis and their persistence in investment.

Not have the right strategies: Most of all have no stable strategies which were correctly verified and fully quantified.

The majority of investors want to look for a secret formula to conquer the stock market. Alternatively, investors want to find a complex system, because they assume that the more complex the system is, the more efficient it is.

However, that is not correct. Lecturers of the University of Finance/ Business (experts in fundamental analysis) who thoroughly understand the complexity of enterprises, theories of stock analysis could not enrich from the stock market, or even have never traded. Alternatively, can we believe in some trading robots or indicators, which are generated from robust computer systems with the complexity of many formulas, algorithms to make money automatically in the stock market?

This book is not merely theoretical, academic, but it contains meticulous analysis and science drawn from practice and verified by the author. The author focuses on analyzing the number of simple contents and rules logically and scientifically, then disclose the two simple strategies for gaining money in the stock market:

The first: Buy stocks according to the portfolio of the largest investment funds. We choose the best active stocks, only buy and hold at the most appropriate general market condition.

The second: Buy and manage best growth stocks, based on the growth investing principles of Jesse Livermore, Nicolas Darvas, William O'Neil... applied scientific methods by using full quantification checklists and eliminating emotion.

The analytical information in this book uses Amibroker graphs and data information from Yahoo Finance. Through the shared analytical content, the readers can thoroughly test and verify to understand the method, and have enough conviction to participate in the market effectively, and achieve success.

If you are a new investor, this book will save you much time in finding simple, practical, effective strategies, and eliminating some unnecessary mistakes. If you are a value investor, this book will help you understand the nature of the market, and why the stocks go up or down. If you are a growth investor, the book will help you understand the nature of strategy, the core principles so that you can complete the process, make the checklist, save much time in routine work.

The book is suitable for both novices and experienced investors. Understanding and applying the contents of this book, the time of stock analyzing, trading decision making, and portfolio management will not exceed 30 minutes per day.

In the process of guiding stock analysis and investment decisions, some information is automatically considered to be correct without detailed or clear explanations. Because of the author's desire to achieve brevity, these points will be further explained in the next several books.

In the process of reading the investment strategies that this book offers, if there are any questions, investors can send queries and seek specific advice via the website: www.bestleadingstocks.com.

Chapter 1: FIRST APPROACHES

1. Fundamental analysis or Technical analysis:

* Analysis Object 1: Enterprise or company

A business or company is understood to be a unit engaged in production, or business activities, bringing products, services or solutions to customers, to make a profit for enterprise and shareholders. We are interested in:

The present value of the enterprise is expressed through business results, financial statements, balance sheet statements, cash flow reports.

The future value of enterprises is reflected through the forecast and expectation of investors on the business results in the future, based on the current business information: products, business opportunities, Board of Directors, market, the current situation of the business, etc.

Analyzing Enterprise: Often used by value investors to search for value stocks. Some other investors also applied the enterprise analysis method to look for growth stocks such as Philip A. Fisher, and Peter Lynch (GARP – growth at a reasonable price). However, they have applied a combination of the "scuttlebutt" technique, direct interviews with competitors, customers, employees, ... or visiting businesses.

Thereby, investors analyze businesses to understand the current activities, opportunities to develop in the future, thus assessing whether the value of stocks has a chance to increase gradually or not.

This analysis type is called "Fundamental analysis" or (FA).

Analysis Object 2: Stock price

The stock has no fixed value and is measured by its price in the market. The investors enthusiastically buy stocks because they believe it is an excellent investment; the stock price will increase. However, if they think the prospects of the company are not bright, and the plan is not to invest more or sell off the stocks, the price of the stock will fall. Stock prices reflect the demand for shares owned by investors (stock supply and demand), or our expectations about the future business results, or some other motive for controlling management rights, even manipulating the stock price.

Researching stock prices is to look at the charts of price and trading volume in one session, in a specific period in order to find historical rules, and evaluate the growth of that stock in comparison with other stocks. According to the chart reading, it is possible to find a chance of success when participating in stock trading.

This analysis type is called "Technical analysis" or (TA).

These two subjects of research, in the short term, do not have a linear relationship, but in a long time enough, they have mutual relations: sustainable growth of enterprises, the stock price will rise. Also, stocks with stable growth prices, enterprises will develop well in the long term.

Which object do you choose to study?

❖ *Selecting only Enterprise analysis (Fundamental Analysis):*

Suitable for organized investors, investors who can understand well the enterprise to seek value stocks. This method needs to study all financial indicators, deeply research the product industry, competitive advantages of businesses, management, strategy....

The risk of this method is: If an economic recession occurs, the market downturn, the investors have to wait for a long time without gaining profit. When making wrong decisions in choosing an enterprise, the results will be hazardous if you don't track the stock prices. Alternatively, if you trust the enterprise excessively, you can buy the whole enterprise over time and get a burden. Because the enterprise is good, the lower the stock price, the more you should buy stock.

❖ *Selecting only stock price analysis (Technical Analysis):*

More suitable for individual investors, who do not have a foundation of financial analysis, and often carry out short-term transactions. These investors use the technical formulas, technical indicators, stock activities models to make the decision to buy and sell stocks.

The risk of this method is the wrong choice of stock or weak enterprises or mistaken application of the indicators or bad indicators. In fact, many indicators have been tested in the past work adequately, but are not capable of predicting the future. The number of indicators is significant, but no indicator is wholly reliable or superior to other indicators. Moreover, each indicator is for one stock, and there is no link to the general market or interaction with other stocks.

The combination of technical analysis and fundamental analysis, with the condition of an uptrend general market, will minimize risks and increase the advantage of both methods, and bring maximum trading efficiency.

2. Investing or trading:

Both investing and trading involve seeking profit by buying and selling stocks, but they pursue that goal in different ways.

❖ **Investing**: Investors often conduct business analysis to determine to buy/ sell stocks, which is called investing. These investors occasionally take profit, and rarely stop loss, because their object is the business, and the goal is the profit of the shareholder in the future. They only liquidate the stock when the operation is no longer according to their expectations. Investors have a longer-term outlook and plan. They often hold shares both in the uptrend or downtrend market.

❖ **Trading**: Investors often analyze the price of the stock to decide to buy/ sell stocks, which is called trading. These investors usually take profit and stop loss to ensure optimal profit for the portfolio and to preserve the account. Traders buy and sell stocks within weeks, days, even minutes, with the aim of short-term gains. They often focus on technical analysis rather than a company's long-term prospects. What matters to traders is which direction the stock will move next and how the trader can profit from that move.

Being different about object analysis and holding time, but investing and trading both have the probability of success - fails when deciding on a buy-sell transaction. No one investor is always right in the market.

If the probability of successful trades is low, the stock liquidation rate is high, the profit of winning trades cannot compensate for the loss of losing trades, the rate of the drawdown of the account balance is not reasonable, investors will not be able to survive on the market.

Chapter 2: LARGE FUNDS CAN SURVIVE AND EXIST FOR A LONG TIME

In the securities market, many mutual funds, exchange-traded funds (ETFs) can survive and grow for a long time. That is why we need to research and learn from them.

Investors liked investing their free money into mutual funds, but now ETFs are taking advantage and increasingly popular, attracting much money from investors.

❖ The reasons that mutual funds, ETFs fund can survive for a long time:
  ➢ There are fund managers with their superior knowledge, experience, and capacity.
  ➢ Holding the backbone businesses of the economy. In the long term, the economy grows, so these funds exist and develop.
❖ Why mutual funds are hard to develop impressively, and the expectation of most joining investors is around the achievement of ETFs or the index's simulation.
  ➢ The funds hold a large amount of money, so they have to allocate their portfolios into many types of stocks, and the average results can hardly be mutated and thrived.

> ➤ Investment funds often hold stocks, including periods of a market downturn, not to be optimal in investment activities. They almost do not plan to convert to keeping cash in challenging market periods.

❖ Can we know the enormous fund's portfolio?

> ➤ You only search by keyword "largest mutual funds," or "largest ETFs" to find the top significant investment funds in the world or one country, and get the results less than 2 seconds.

> ➤ Investment funds make public their investment portfolios on investment fund management companies' websites, or they inform on financial news websites.

> ➤ It is not difficult to find the top 20-30 favorite stocks, which are in the portfolio of these funds, mostly blue-chip stocks, or large companies' stocks, acting as the backbone of the national economy.

At this point, by the advantage of individual investors, we can jump in and out very fast with the favorite stocks from the portfolio of the most significant funds. However, it is crucial to remember that we only follow them at a good general market condition, while the bad general market situation, we keep cash patiently waiting for opportunities.

We have the No. 1 lesson about the simple investment strategy. The necessary and sufficient conditions: 1. Copy and follow huge funds; 2. Uptrend market after the recession. Details of the strategy will be presented in detail in chapter 6.

Chapter 3: GROWTH INVESTING STRATEGY HELPS MANY FAMOUS INVESTORS BECOME RICH

F inding value stocks are often getting profit, a high probability of success in a recovery market period after the downturn happened. At a growth market period, looking for the advantage of value stocks is not a wise solution; otherwise, the risk is much more than the opportunity. That urges investors to find growth stocks and make efforts to develop growth stock trading methods.

What is the growth stock? In a simple explanation, they are the stocks of the enterprises whose business results, annual revenue, and annual earnings grow continuously. The prices of these stocks surged more than the average of the general market and outperformed much more than the average of the sector/ industry. The stock price regularly grows over time, without selling off and divesting activities by big investors.

There are two ways of analytical methods to search growth stocks which are verified in history and applied till now:

1. Fundamental analysis and extended questions:

Successfully summarized and used by Philip Fisher, the best American stock investor as the author of Common Stocks and Uncommon Profits.

15

The book still has been remaining in print ever since it was first published in 1958.

Peter Lynch was known as the successful growth investor. He often went for field checking, talking to BOD, and trying on the products, services of the company. He has been looking for a better price chance to buy by concept (GARP – growth at a reasonable price).

The method focuses on fundamental analysis of enterprise and extended information related to businesses. Including:

❖ Analyzing business activities, financial activities in detail.
❖ Using the "scuttlebutt" method, interviewing, or field check on products/ services of the company: Understanding businesses through customers, competitors, banks, partners, suppliers....
❖ Offering a set of 15 questions to look for extraordinary stocks, related to products, product potentials, management team, sales organizing, profit margins, etc.

2. Methods of combining fundamental analysis and technical analysis:

Successfully applied by Bernard Baruch, Jesse Livermore, Gerald Loeb, Nicolas Darvas, O'Neil. When the information technology industry developed, this method was further improved by some investors with strong computer support; they even built information consulting platforms for customers. The number of investors applying this method is enormous, and many succeeded. The main analytical criteria of this method include:

❖ The general market movements: only participate in the uptrend market (considered only by technical analysis).
❖ Stock's technical analysis items: Stock with strength index in comparison with itself in history; the stock price increase in comparison with the general market or other stocks; the volume of the inflow from organized investors.

❖ Enterprises have an excellent fundamental analysis score: sustainable growth business and recent sudden growth earning. It is understood that business results in the last three years stably grow (reflected by yearly Revenue, Earnings, EPS), high ROE; and by quarter, Revenue, Earnings increased significantly recently.

In the above two ways, the fundamental analysis combined with the technical analysis method has more advantages, higher quantification, easer application, and of course, better efficiency. Find the answer for the quantitative questions will be more comfortable and more evident for every investor, not only for the professional investors. Moreover, Philip Fisher's method also ignores the general market trend while this is one of the essential factors affecting the possibility of stock selection or the accuracy of stock purchasing decisions.

We have the No. 2 lesson about the simple investment strategy. The necessary and sufficient conditions: 1. An uptrend of the general market, select and manage the best growth stock, 2. Stably developing enterprises, and earnings speed up recently. Details of the strategy will be presented in detail in chapter 7.

17

Chapter 4: CAN WE BEAT UP THE STOCK MARKET

❖ *Typically, the average win/ loss ratio is 50%*

You did not use any analysis method to choose a stock. You used the dart, targeted to the nameplate, and selected the stock that the arrow does. You bought those stocks. Then you forgot, did not read information, did not trade. One day you remember that you own the stock. You sell it. You have a probability of 50% profit, 50% loss. That is an average win/loss ratio.

So, you can increase or decrease your win/loss ratio depending on additional analysis factors, and your emotions that you can control.

❖ *World economic, backbone companies go up for the long term*

Talking about the economic situation, the economy of the countries always moves continuously. Despite bleak periods sometimes, in the long term, growth always goes up. Therefore, along with stock market scores, many stocks will grow and grow over time.

Figure 4-1: Dow Jones Industrial Average (^DJI), 1990-2018, weekly chart

Figure 4-2: Microsoft Corporation (MSFT)1990-2019, daily chart

Figure 4-3: Apple, Inc. (AAPL) 1998-2019, daily chart

❖ *Money flows mainly between investors, not run much into the broker company*

Besides brokerage fees to be paid to brokers, tax at a low rate, most of the amount of profit/loss will be transferred among investors. Therefore, if we practice a smarter investment method than others, profits will run into our pockets.

❖ *70% of stocks go up or down following the general market*

There is the fact that 70% of stocks will increase/decrease according to general market movements, as the S&P 500, Dow Jones, Nasdaq. Therefore, if you own stocks in the period of the uptrend market, you have a 70% chance of earning profits.

❖ *Good stocks have "good" traits both FA and TA*

(FA) Excellent enterprises, good stocks will be the target of professional investment funds. When huge funds disbursed to buy stocks, we can thoroughly read by the trading volume, or published information of businesses, or newsletters on financial websites.

(TA) Technical analysis is another filter to improve accuracy when deciding to buy stocks. Successful stocks will surely have successful characteristics. Moreover, considering the movements carefully in the price chart, investors will judge logically about the movement of the stock.

❖ *The mathematical principle helps us understand clearly about stock market operating.*

> ➢ Market index $= \Sigma(\text{market cap})/\text{divisor}$

> ➢ Market index $\sim$ the price of each stock

(All market, or group of specific stocks)
Symbol explanations:
"~": proportional relationship

Σ: total

We consider in one period and assume the index is increasing.

> ➢ Market index ~ (the price of each stock in group No.1) & (the price of each stock in group No.2)

❖ Group No.1: Each member of group No.1 is stronger than the index and goes up higher than the index does since the specific date (R.S of each member of group No.1 >= R.S of the index).

❖ Group No.2: Each member of group No.2 is weaker than the index and goes down or goes up slower than the index does since the specific date (R.S of each member of group No.2 < R.S of the index).

(R.S: Relative Strength, read more in Chapter 5, Item No. 3)

Group No.1 supports the market to go up, in contrast to group No.2, pulling the market down.

In the bull (uptrend) market, stocks in Group No.1 tend to continue to stay in group No.1, to support the market continue to go up and keep the uptrend status.

So, if we know and control well stocks of Group No.1, we have a significant opportunity to win in the stock market.

In summary, there are many facilities, many principles to improve the probability of random stock selection (chance of winning 50%), to a higher 70%, or 80%. Therefore, we can win in the stock market.

Chapter 5: TECHNICAL ANALYSIS

1. Many indicators are tricking:

There are many indicators to support technical analysis when analyzing Stocks, Forex, or Cryptocurrencies, the number up to several hundred. Typically, there are some indicators: SMA (Simple Moving Average), EMA (Exponential Moving Average), MFI (Money Flow Index), MACD, PSAR (Parabolic SAR), SS (Slow Stochastic), FS (Fast Stochastic), ...

Indicators are also available on many platforms, be normative, and become standard tools in all trading platforms, e.g., Amibroker, MetaTrader, Tradingview, some applications on android phones, or iOS.

We do not mention more about their convenience and diversity, but if they are useful or superior, then the question is, why there are so many indicators? Indeed, if they can help us survive in the stock market, just using 1-2 indicators can make us satisfied.

In my opinion, there are some reasons why they are not useful:

❖ They are secondary tools interpolated. It may be true in a specific situation, but it is not always true. Take an example like this. We go to the doctor. The doctor will rely on symptoms, primary analysis results (ultrasound results, X-ray results, blood tests) to conclude the patient's condition, and give solutions. However, if using a machine doctor (like an indicator) instead of a human doctor, can you trust to hear the conclusion, and follow the treatment regimen from that machine doctor?

❖ Primary tools are Price and Volume. That will be two crucial parameters we shall care about, instead of secondary indicators that are not highly accurate.

❖ The indicator itself mostly relies on price fluctuations only. There may be very few, or as far as I know, there is no indicator that has a combination of Price and Volume, and the interactions between stocks, or with the general market.

Above told are the reasons why the indicator is almost a representation, not a practical application. Similarly, we study Karate, we practice "Form" - KATA, practice "Sparring" - KUMITE, or drill "Strength, Reaction" then "Form" is almost for impressive performances and basic technique, but less effective in competition.

In the stock market, many indicators that reflect the past very correctly, very accurately, but they are not capable of correctly drawing for the future; these are the "repainting indicators" only. That is tricking.

Moreover, when applying the indicators, we do not fully understand the author's intention. We also don't understand which formulas, algorithms are hidden, and what are the exclusion factors behind the code.

In general, these free tools hardly help us to be satisfied.

Besides, referring to patterns, for example, Cup-with-Handle, Double Bottom, Flat Base, etc. They are similar to indicators; however, it is more complicated to use or find out the correct pattern, or automatic programming detected in some trading platforms.

The author does not recommend using indicators, as well as patterns on analyzing and evaluating stocks.

2. Using only the most simple parameters and indicators:

Basing on the explanations above, the author suggests using only some primary parameters, and indicators as follow:

a. Chart type and data:

❖ Price: bar type, OHLC (Open, High, Low, Close).
❖ Volume: histogram type.

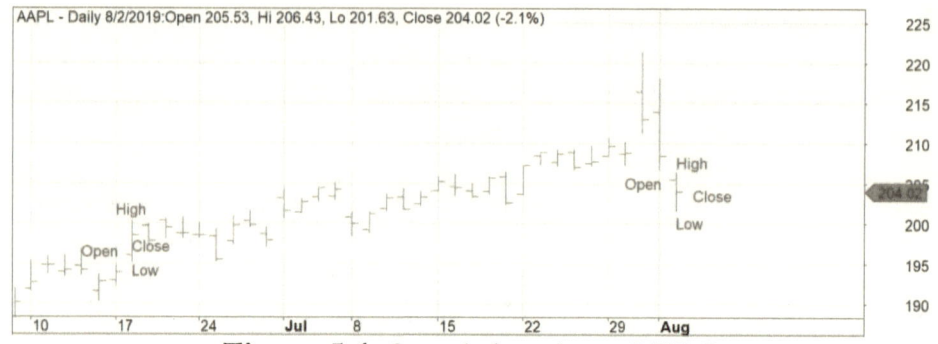

Figure 5-1: Sample bar chart, OHLC

❖ Data: EOD (end of day), or intraday delayed data is good enough to use. Do not need to use real-time data, or minute, hourly chart.

b. Indicators:

❖ MA10: used in Price pane
❖ EMA9: used in Volume pane

c. Platform:

Recommended to use Amibroker and data source, read more:
http://www.amibroker.com/guide/h_quotes.html.

Figure 5-2: Bar chart price + MA10, Volume + EMA9

3. Strength of Stock:

Investors may know some concepts of stock strength indexes such as RS (Relative strength), or RSI (Relative strength index). They are technique tools, calculations that can compare the performance of a stock to the overall market or to itself.

However, there are many formulas, calculations that cause you to be confused about usage and profound meaning.

Within this book, the author gives two strength indexes:

❖ **Intrinsic Strength (I.S):** to evaluate the strength of stock and compare it to itself in history, usually be reviewed within one year back from the current date. It is long enough to reflect the movement of the stock price in one business year, the buying and selling demand of the funds or investors. That expresses the mindset and the stability of investors' mood.

Suggested formula:

I.S = EOD price/ highest close price in one year

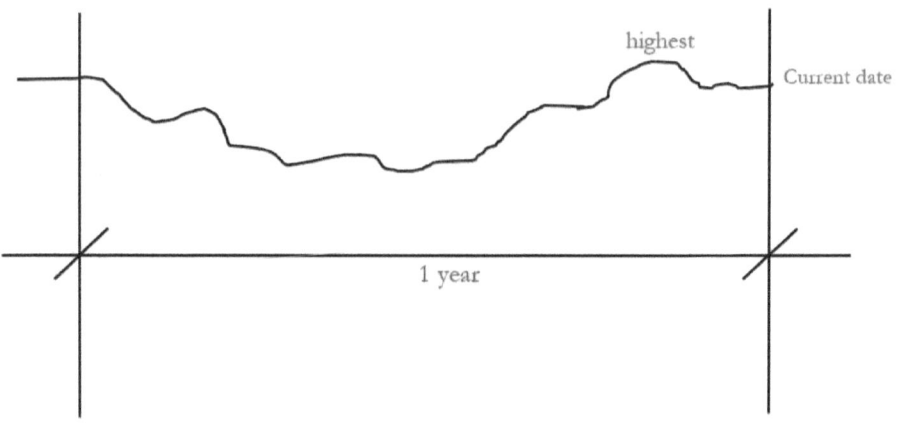

Figure 5-3: Chart and I.S calculation

Figure 5-4: KO – daily chart, and a sample of I.S calculation

I.S = EOD price/ highest close price in one year
I.S of KO (8/2/2019) = 52.33/54.33 = 0.963.

❖ **Relative Strength (R.S):** To evaluate the relative strength of stock and compare to other stocks, or the general market represented by Dow Jones (^ DJI), S & P500 (^ GSPC), Nasdaq (^ IXIC), etc.

During the uptrend market period, if the stock price increases more strongly than the general market, the R.S of stock will be higher than the R.S of the general market, because it is contributing to pulling up the general market score.

Suggested formula:

R.S = EOD price / close price of the market bottom day.

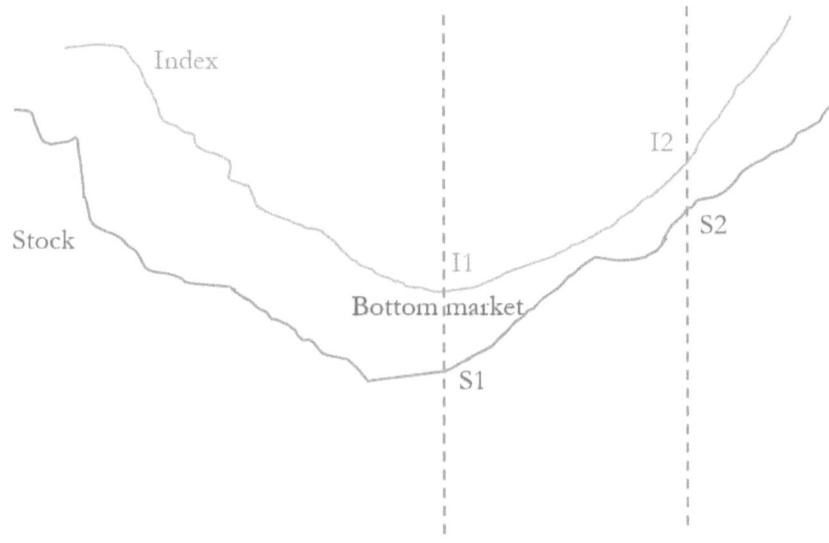

Figure 5-5: Compare R.S of Stock to R.S of Index

➢ R.S of the index: I2/ I1*100 (%)
➢ R.S of stock: S2/S1*100 (%)

When we buy blue-chip stocks that ETFs, Mutual funds hold much, we only need to check out the R.S without caring about the I.S, as the businesses are the backbone.

When we buy growth stocks, we shall check out both the I.S and the R.S to ensure the safety and the highest probability of success. A high I.S index shows the support cashflow of old investors; a high R.S index shows the support cashflow of new investors.

Chapter 6: STRATEGY 1 – BUY STOCKS ACCORDING TO THE PORTFOLIO OF THE LARGEST INVESTMENT FUNDS

✓ *Necessary condition: Follow the most significant funds' portfolios*
✓ *Sufficient condition: Uptrend general market after the recession period.*

This lesson provides a simple, safe, effective investment method, but the expected profit is not really high; it is impossible to implement regular investment because favorable market opportunities do not often happen.

Why is this method safe and effective?

Firstly, substantial mutual funds, ETFs can live for the long term. Therefore, the major stocks in their portfolio are sure for safe and profitable. The funds have researched and selected the qualified enterprises, and these are the large ones with stability, large capitalization, high liquidity in selling if necessary. However, we only choose some of the most active gainers (having the strongest R.S) in the uptrend general market after a recession. Within the period, it is sure of the highest chance of success. The most active stocks will lead the general market to go up, and then the market spreads to the other stocks.

The wining opportunity is 80-90%.

1. Strategy and explanation:

a. Create and update the watching list (Stocks are qualified by Large Funds):

The enormous mutual funds, ETFs will hold outstanding stock tickers, which have confirmed the quality of the business, the quality of the stocks, the ability to grow sustainably and the chance to increase the price. However, the characteristics of these tickers are quite "heavy," strongly influenced by the general market trend.

There is a concept called "Coattail investment," which is a method to copy the list of prominent investors such as Warren Buffett, George Soros, ... Thus, our approach is not new. Significant investment funds often actively share their portfolio information with the public. According to the regulation of The 1933 Securities Act, funds of over $ 100 million must be registered with the Securities and Exchange Commission (SEC), and share their portfolio information regularly.

Therefore, it is not difficult to find out the list of stock held by the most significant investment funds.

Searching a few phrases as "largest mutual funds" or "largest ETFs" on Google.com, you will find the listed fund right away.

largest etf

🔍 All 📰 News 📷 Images ▶ Videos ⋮ More   Settings Tools

About 28,900,000 results (0.56 seconds)

10 Biggest ETFs of 2018 By Total Market Capitalization

- SPDR S&P 500 **ETF** (SPY) -- $241.61 Billion. ...
- iShares Core S&P 500 ETF (IVV) -- $144.49 Billion. ...
- Vanguard Total Stock Market ETF (VTI) -- $93.76 Billion. ...
- Vanguard S&P 500 **ETF** (VOO) -- $93.36 Billion. ...
- Vanguard FTSE Developed Markets **ETF** (VEA) -- $65.18 Billion. ...
- iShares MSCI EAFE **ETF** (EFA) -- $61.66 Billion.

Dec 20, 2018

10 Biggest ETFs of 2018 By Total Market Capitalization - Yahoo Finance
https://finance.yahoo.com/news/10-biggest-etfs-2018-total-182848079.html

ⓘ About this result   ▨ Feedback

Largest ETFs: Top 100 ETFs By Assets | ETF Database
https://etfdb.com/compare/market-cap/ ▾
Largest ETFs: Top 100 ETFs By Assets. The following table lists the top 100 largest exchange-traded
funds, ranked by assets under management (AUM).
You've visited this page 3 times. Last visit: 7/5/19

Largest ETFs by Assets Under Management (AUM) - The Balance
https://www.thebalance.com › Investing › ETFs › Basics ▾
Unlike their mutual fund cousins. ETFs that have the highest amount of money invested in them can
have advantages over ETFs that have lower assets under management. A mutual fund's net assets
under management, or AUM. not to be confused with Net Asset Value (NAV). represents the ...
You've visited this page 3 times. Last visit: 7/30/19

Google   largest mutual fund   🎤 🔍

🔍 All 📷 Images 📰 News ▶ Videos ⋮ More   Settings Tools

About 53,600,000 results (0.56 seconds)

The 25 Largest Mutual Funds

Rank	Symbol	Fund Name
1	SPY	SPDR S&P 500 ETF
2	VFIAX	Vanguard 500 Idx Adm
3	VTSAX	Vanguard TSM Idx Adm
4	FXAIX	Fidelity 500 Index Fund

21 more rows

The 25 Largest Mutual Funds - MarketWatch
https://www.marketwatch.com/tools/mutual-fund/top25largest

ⓘ About this result   ▨ Feedback

People also ask

Which is the largest mutual fund group in the world?   ⌄

What are the top 10 mutual funds?   ⌄

What mutual fund has the highest return?   ⌄

What is the largest ETF?   ⌄

Feedback

The 25 Largest Mutual Funds - MarketWatch
https://www.marketwatch.com/tools/mutual-fund/top25largest
A New Watchlist. We've updated Watchlist! The changes include a new. responsive design featuring

Figure 6-1: Search funds in google.com

Typing the names of these investment funds on financial website pages, such as https://finance.yahoo.com/, or https://www.marketwatch.com/, we quickly find the stocks they hold the most.

At a glance, our strategy is seeming similar to the coattail investment funds by copying the portfolio of the significant investment funds. But, the nature of the strategy, buy method, and sell method is totally different. The coattail investments are often passive investors; they copied the trading activities of stocks from investment funds, and often hold stocks for a long time. As for our strategy, just "taking advantage" of the stock lists qualified by significant investment funds, we actively buy at the most appropriate time and sell according to the mathematical principles.

❖ *How to do:*
  ➤ *Search the name of the largest funds, and check which stocks they are holding the most.*
  ➤ *Find the list of top 30 stocks that the largest ETFs and mutual funds hold the most.*
  ➤ *Update the list every month (watching list)*

b. *Opportunity from the general market (Only Technical analysis):*

❖ *Chance after the recession period:*

When the market was on the downturn, everything was sold out violently. The market index has dropped significantly. Stocks are sold more than usual, many stocks and indexes are "very cheap, very low" and falling to the bottom.

This period is an investment opportunity for most of the value investors, even a bit blind because they often rush to buy early without knowing what the "bottom" is, and what is the stop of the downtrend market period. As long as they find a "margin of safety" or low enough PE value, they can join early. That shows the attraction of the post-recession market like the glimmering sun drops after the prolonged dark rain.

However, as a growth investor, we must find the bottom of a short period, before the market starts to turn up. The short-term bottom is assumed to be within 3 to 7 days before, since that day, the market started going up, and there was no day with the closing price lower than that assumption.

In general, the market recovers after the recession, everything is in pink, hundreds of flowers bloom. It can be said that 70-80% of the stocks increase price daily. Our mission is to calm down, identify the bottom of the market, confirm the up-channel market signal, choose qualified and leading stocks, which are contributing to increase the market index.

To be called the recession periods, indexes should decrease at least by 17% from the nearest peak, and the downtrend time lasts more than three months. After that period, the market goes up by the significant contribution from blue-chip stocks, the large-cap stocks, which the investment funds hold. In this period, the asset value of investment funds usually grows well, sticking to general market indexes.

❖ *Look for uptrend market signal after recession period:*

The thorough and compulsory principle I want to mention here is to wait for the market going past the downturn, to find the bottom day, and the confirmed up-channel before deciding to join the market.

Content of considering and determining the uptrend market is presented in Chapter 7, item No. 3.

Be noted that the general market review is to look at the indexes (^ DJI, ^ GSPC, ^ IXIC) at daily closing.

❖ *How to do:*

➢ *Find the bottom day (based on EOD - end of day point of the index). That is a hypothetical bottom day, appearing at least three days before. Counting from the bottom day, the closing price of all the following days are always higher than this bottom. If this bottom is broken, the process of finding the bottom day is reset.*

➢ *Find the uptrend confirmation day: After three days or more from the bottom day, appearing the day whose closing price is higher than MA10, and having up-channel confirmation sign, and indexes' R.S higher than 2.5%.*

From this day, we can start to buy stocks. When we consider buying stocks, we need to check to ensure the market maintain the up-channel, and above MA10.

c. How to buy (Only Technical analysis):

Creating the watch list helps us to refine and find the qualified stocks; furthermore, these stocks are "supported" by significant investment funds. By buying these stocks, we eliminate unforeseen risks or even bankruptcy if any. However, randomly choosing to buy any stock, at any time, will not bring a satisfactory result, or also suffer decreased account, in case of unfortunately selecting the weakest stocks.

We all want to beat the market, earn good profits and minimum risks. That is the reason we need to find the best opportunity and the most appropriate "general market" condition. And, the more important is finding stocks with the best increase opportunities.

We are going back to the question: "Which came first: the chicken or the egg?", similar to "Which increase first? The general market or stock? ". The second question is more comfortable to answer.

According to the author, when the market oversells, buying will be started from some stocks that have "nice stories"(business results, internal information, innovation, products, or other motivations). Professional investors will go ahead. The stocks that are bought much enough will pull the market up; after the market goes up, it will continue to pull up the stocks. Both will lead each other up until the next downturn happens, and investors take profit, ending a wave cycle.

Therefore, when there are signs of up-channel confirmation, we need to find the strongest increased stocks and stronger than the general market. They are wings to lift the general market. The stocks containing a beautiful story, or something like "the smart money," or a "secret reason" will have the best opportunities to increase in the soonest.

The strength or weakness rating is R.S of stock (Review Chapter 5, item No.3). We calculate R.S of all stocks in watching list from the bottom day till consideration date, compare among these stocks' R.S to R.S of the general market. Rank the stocks according to their R.S from high to low and select the top R.S members.

❖ *How to do:*
  ➤ *Select from the above watching list.*
  ➤ *Calculate R.S of stock, and rank them from largest to smallest.*
  ➤ *Choose the stocks whose R.S are on top to buy.*

d. How to Sell (Only Technical analysis):

The purpose of stock trading is profit, after deciding to hold stocks, we need to manage "selling" to ensure the best chance of gains, risk limitation, and avoiding a capital backlog.

Selling is considered to be much more complicated than buying. Many investors, especially growth investors, believe that it is quite cumbersome and compulsory to use complicated analysis methods to decide. It would be a pity if the stock we just sold can take off. It would also be sad if we do not decisively sell out early; keep holding stock so long that we dare not look at the account.

Price increasing needs many reasons, but price decreasing needs no more than one. Everything reflects in price; that is why we manage to sell stocks only by technical analysis. If we wait for something relating to "fundamental analysis," that is too late.

We have four selling scenarios:

❖ **Sell to take profit**: With historical data, as well as expectations of most investors, the market is possible to recover after the recession period. The expected profit-taking level is set at 15% higher than the price of the uptrend confirmation date.

❖ **Sell to cut loss:** According to the TP / SL ratio of 3/1, as well as the characteristics of price changing of blue-chip, the stock price is challenging to recover right after occurring 5-7% reduction. Therefore, the author warns you to cut loss if the price is 5% lower than the price at the up-channel confirmation date.

❖ **Liquidation:** Although the stock does not reach the TP or the SL value, we should consider about liquidation if one of the two cases below happens:

  ➢ The general market breaks the up-channel, and under the MA10 line, risks come from the general market.

  ➢ The R.S of stocks are smaller than the R.S of the general market: The stocks do not support the market anymore.

❖ **Emergency selling:** Emergency selling is like activating "autopilot" mode, or emergency injection case in medicine. The author warns that in case of the stocks suddenly drop by 10% or more during a trading session, we shall activate the emergency selling mode on the trading system, or through the broker company without delay.

Emergency selling is an essential technique in response to unexpected situations, such as war, politics, etc. If you delay on liquidating stocks, you may suffer serious consequences.

2. Some examples in the real market (testing):

I. *Strong downtrend (recession) from 10/3/2018 to 12/24/2018, uptrend later from 12/24/2018 to 2/25/2019:*

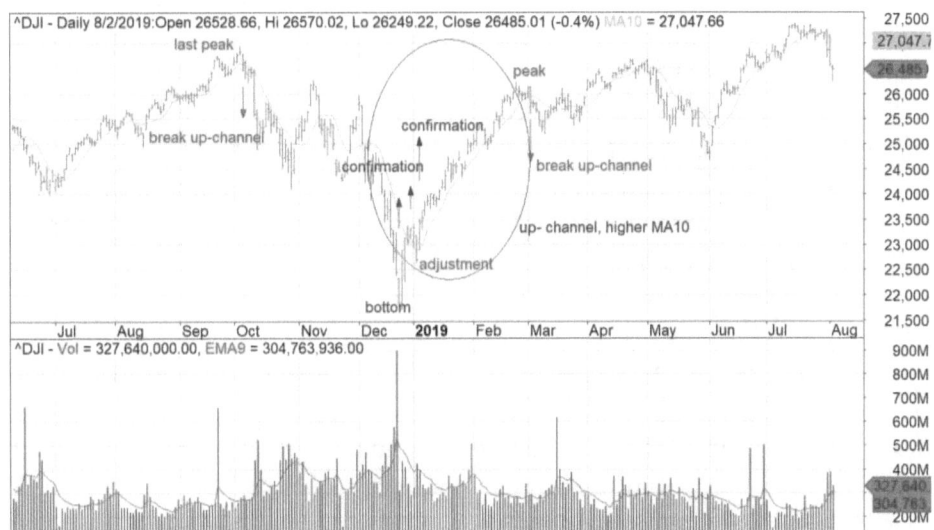

Figure 6-2: Dow Jones Industrial Average (^DJI), 2018-2019, daily chart, illustrates bottom, peak, in/out date

a. *Watching list:*

See which Mutual Funds, or ETFs are the biggest: Vanguard 500 Index Fund Admiral Shares (VFIAX), Vanguard Total Stock Market Index Fund Admiral Shares (VTSAX), Fidelity 500 Index Fund (FXAIX), SPDR S&P 500 ETF (SPY), iShares Core S&P 500 ETF (IVV), Vanguard S&P 500 ETF (VOO), ...

❖ We get the watching list, including:

Coca-Cola Co ORD; Intel Corp ORD; Merck & Co Inc ORD; UnitedHealth Group Inc ORD; Home Depot Inc ORD; Cisco Systems

Inc ORD; Chevron Corp ORD; Verizon Communications Inc ORD; Mastercard Inc ORD; Pfizer Inc ORD; Walt Disney Co ORD; AT&T Inc ORD; Bank of America Corp ORD; Procter & Gamble Co ORD; Visa Inc ORD; Exxon Mobil Corp ORD; Alphabet Inc ORD; JPMorgan Chase & Co ORD; Johnson & Johnson ORD; Berkshire Hathaway Inc ORD; Facebook Inc ORD; Amazon.com Inc ORD; Apple Inc ORD; Microsoft Corp ORD.

With a bit of lazy, we will use the list of stocks in ^ DJI (Dow Jones Industrial Average) - 30 stocks, ^ DJT (Dow Jones Transportation Average) - 20 stocks, ^ DJU (Dow Jones Utility Average) - 15 stocks, totally 65 stocks are in the watching list. This simple operation brings us a list of the qualified stocks which are "supported" by large investment funds, institutional funds. The qualification criteria also meet the principle of strategy.

You'll see the list of 65 stocks in the three Dow Jones index groups as follows (the list updated 05Aug2019): VZ - Verizon Communications Inc.; JNJ - Johnson & Johnson; KO - The Coca-Cola Company; MRK - Merck & Co., Inc.; CVX - Chevron Corporation; DOW - Dow Inc.; MCD - McDonald's Corporation; UNH - UnitedHealth Group Incorporated; TRV - The Travelers Companies, Inc.; XOM - Exxon Mobil Corporation; CAT - Caterpillar Inc.; DIS - The Walt Disney Company; BA - The Boeing Company; NKE - NIKE, Inc.; PFE - Pfizer Inc.; PG - The Procter & Gamble Company; AXP - American Express Company; JPM - JPMorgan Chase & Co.; WMT - Walmart Inc.; WBA - Walgreens Boots Alliance, Inc.; HD - The Home Depot, Inc.; MMM - 3M Company; MSFT - Microsoft Corporation; INTC - Intel Corporation; CSCO - Cisco Systems, Inc.; GS - The Goldman Sachs Group, Inc.; UTX - United Technologies Corporation; IBM - International Business Machines Corporation; V - Visa Inc.; AAPL - Apple Inc.; CHRW - C.H. Robinson Worldwide, Inc.; JBLU - JetBlue Airways Corporation; NSC - Norfolk Southern Corporation; UPS - United Parcel Service, Inc.; CAR - Avis Budget Group, Inc.; ALK - Alaska Air Group, Inc.; LSTR - Landstar System, Inc.; CSX - CSX Corporation; AAL - American Airlines Group Inc.; LUV - Southwest Airlines Co.; R - Ryder System, Inc.; KEX - Kirby Corporation; DAL - Delta Air Lines, Inc.; UNP - Union Pacific

Corporation; FDX - FedEx Corporation; UAL - United Airlines Holdings, Inc.; KSU - Kansas City Southern; JBHT - J.B. Hunt Transport Services, Inc.; EXPD - Expeditors International of Washington, Inc.; MATX - Matson, Inc.; EXC - Exelon Corporation; ED - Consolidated Edison, Inc.; AEP - American Electric Power Company, Inc.; DUK - Duke Energy Corporation; NEE - NextEra Energy, Inc.; AWK - American Water Works Company, Inc.; EIX - Edison International; D - Dominion Energy, Inc.; FE - FirstEnergy Corp.; PEG - Public Service Enterprise Group Incorporated; SO - The Southern Company; CNP - CenterPoint Energy, Inc.; AES - The AES Corporation; PCG - PG&E Corporation; NI - NiSource Inc.

b. Check the general market:

❖ **Check recession of the general market:**
   ➤ From 10/3/2018 to 12/24/2018, the recession period lasted around 3 months.
   ➤ Rate of decline:
      • ^DJI: from 26,828.39 down to 21,792.2, down rate of: 18.77%
      • ^GSPC: down rate of 19.63%
      • ^IXIC: down rate of 22.83%
   ⇨ **The market plunged enough, equivalent to the recession as the strategy.**
❖ **Look for uptrend market confirmation signal:**
   ➤ <u>**12/24/2018: the bottom day.**</u>
   ➤ <u>**12/31/2018: the confirmation day**</u>, the fourth day since the bottom day, ^DJI: 23,327.46 > MA10 (23,009.66), up 7.0% higher than the bottom day, up-channel signal. Starting from this day, we can consider buying stocks.
   ➤ **01/03/2019: strong adjustment**, under MA10 line, breaking up-channel, we stop buying and take care portfolio.

> ➢ **01/04/2019: the confirmation day again.** Confirmation to continue holding and buying.

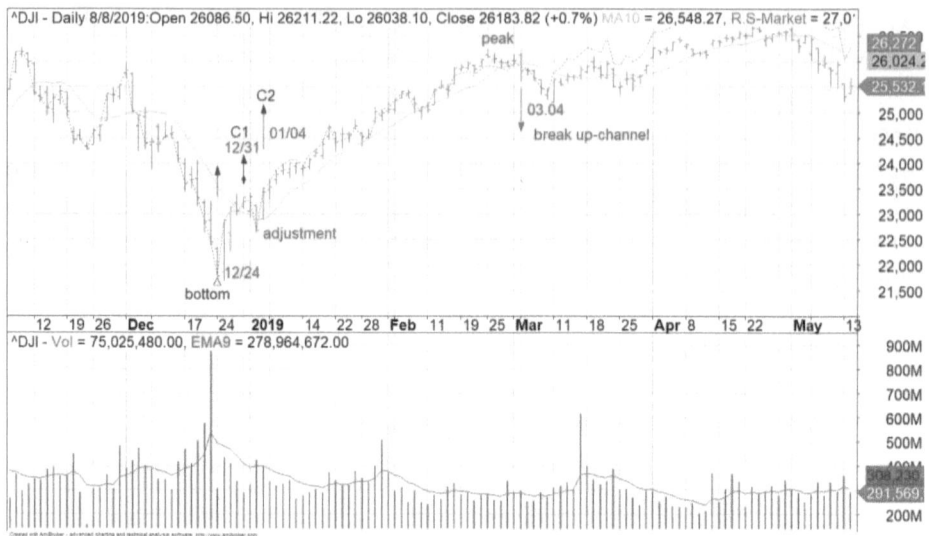

Figure 6-3: Dow Jones Industrial Average (^DJI), 2018-2019, daily chart, one detail uptrend period.

> ➢ Market uptrend lasted until 03/04/2019: under the MA10 line, breaking up-channel. We should sell all the stock on that day.

c.   How to Buy and Sell:

❖ Use the list of 65 stocks from ^DJI, ^DJT, ^DJU as the watching list.
❖ Find stock whose R.S >= R.S of the general market (^DJI, ^GSPC, ^IXIC), and rank the stocks from the largest to the smallest.

✦ **On 12/31/2018, we have the list as below:**
  • R.S of general market at 12/31/2018 = Max R.S (^DJI, ^GSPC, ^IXIC) = 7.1% (of ^IXIC).

- Make the filter, and rank, we have the list in the below table.

Ticker	Date/Time	C	%C/C-1	Vol/EMA9	B.O	Evaluate	Type	>Ma10	I.S	R.S	%	%Date-BottomMarket	%Date-Confirmation	%BreakUpChannel-Confirmation
BA	12/31/2018	322.50	1.9	0.8				1	0.82	9.6		9.6	0.0	34.2
DIS	12/31/2018	109.65	2.2	0.9				1	0.92	9.3		9.3	0.0	4.3
NKE	12/31/2018	74.14	1.1	0.6				1	0.87	8.9		9.8	0.0	15.5
CAT	12/31/2018	127.07	1.2	0.7				1	0.74	8.7		8.7	0.0	8.9
HD	12/31/2018	171.82	0.9	0.7				1	0.80	8.7		8.7	0.0	7.0
WMT	12/31/2018	93.15	1.1	0.7				1	0.85	8.5		8.5	0.0	5.0
UPS	12/31/2018	97.53	1.0	0.6				1	0.73	8.5		8.5	0.0	13.3
V	12/31/2018	131.94	0.8	0.7				1	0.87	8.4		8.4	0.0	12.1
AAL	12/31/2018	32.11	0.9	0.7				1	0.55	8.0		8.0	0.0	5.0
MSFT	12/31/2018	101.57	1.2	0.7				1	0.88	7.9		7.9	0.0	10.5
EXPD	12/31/2018	68.09	2.6	1.1				1	0.87	7.9		7.9	0.0	10.6
UNP	12/31/2018	138.23	1.1	0.7				1	0.84	7.8		7.8	0.0	21.1
KEX	12/31/2018	67.36	1.3	0.7				1	0.72	7.8		8.1	0.0	10.7
INTC	12/31/2018	46.93	0.4	0.7				1	0.82	7.7		7.7	0.0	14.9
CVX	12/31/2018	108.79	0.1	0.7				1	0.81	7.7		7.7	0.0	12.3
PFE	12/31/2018	43.65	1.6	0.7				1	0.94	7.6		7.6	0.0	-1.3
CSCO	12/31/2018	43.33	1.3	0.7				1	0.88	7.6		7.6	0.0	18.1
AAPL	12/31/2018	157.74	1.0	0.7				1	0.68	7.4		7.4	0.0	11.5
MRK	12/31/2018	76.41	1.4	0.6				1	0.96	7.4		7.4	0.0	6.5

Figure 6-4: Ranked list on 12/31/2018 of stocks whose R.S >= R.S of the general market, the bottom day: 12/24/2018

In the table, you can see the last column named "%BreakUpChannel-Confirmation" which is the percentage of profit or loss at break up-channel day compare to the confirmation day of that stock. All stocks get profit, except PFE get loss 1.3%

The detail of some stocks:

1. The Boeing Company (BA):

Figure 6-5: Daily chart, BA (Boeing Company) 2017-2019

➤ Be a successful stock.
➤ To be able to take profit at 15%, even 34.2% until break the up-channel day (03/04/2019).
➤ R.S of stock always > R.S of the general market.
➤ No emergency sell signal.

2. The Walt Disney Company (DIS):

Figure 6-6: Daily chart, DIS (Walt Disney Company) 2017-2019

➢ Not a successful stock.
➢ Be sold on 1/16/2019, because of its R.S < R.S of the general market, profit at 1.1%.
➢ No emergency sell signal.

3. NIKE, Inc. (NKE):

NKE - Daily 12/31/2018:Open 73.98, Hi 74.46, Lo 73.52, Close 74.14 (+1.1%) MA10 = 71.22, R.S-Market = 72.61

NKE - Vol = 5,519,100.00, EMA9 = 9,287,093.00

Figure 6-7: Daily chart, NIKE (Nike, Inc.) 2017-2019

> ➢ Be a successful stock.
> ➢ To be able to take profit at 15%, even 15.5% until the break up-channel day (03/04/2019).
> ➢ R.S of stock always > R.S of the general market.
> ➢ No emergency sell signal.

4. We draw the chart and check all stocks according to the list above, for 19 stocks: BA, DIS, NKE, CAT, HD, WMT, UPS, V, AAL, MSFT, EXPD, KEX, UNP, CVX, INTC, CSCO, PFE, AAPL, MRK (the list of stocks on 12/31/2018).

✦ **On the next days: From this date to 03/04/2019, we check the R.S of all stock in watching list (65 stocks) belonging to the Dow Jones above every day, and consider selling if the stocks' R.S is lower than the R.S of the general market. In case the stocks' R.S maintain higher than the general market's R.S, and be on the top, they will be successful stocks.**

✦ **During the period from 12/31/2018 to 03/04/2019, the stocks were successful (meeting the condition of taking profit at 15%):**

Ticker	Name	Nice Buy Date	I.S on Buy Date	R.S on Buy Date	Take Profit 15%	%BreakUpChannel-Confirmation
BA	Boeing Company (The)	12/31/2018	0.82	9.6	TP15	34.2
NKE	Nike, Inc.	12/31/2018	0.87	8.9	TP15	15.5
UNP	Union Pacific Corporation	12/31/2018	0.84	7.8	TP15	21.1
KEX	Kirby Corporation	12/31/2018	0.72	7.8	TP15	10.7
CSCO	Cisco Systems, Inc.	12/31/2018	0.88	7.6	TP15	18.1
GS	Goldman Sachs Group, Inc. (The)	1/2/2019	0.63	10	TP15	17.3
R	Ryder System, Inc.	1/2/2019	0.54	8.1	TP15	30
IBM	International Business Machines Corporation	1/3/2019	0.67	5	TP15	21.8
XOM	Exxon Mobil Corporation	1/3/2019	0.77	4.7	TP15	17.8
LSTR	Landstar System, Inc.	1/7/2019	0.79	10.3	TP15	12.3
NSC	Norfolk Souther Corporation	1/8/2019	0.84	12.1	TP15	20.2
CAR	Avis Budget Group, Inc.	1/10/2019	0.51	14.3	TP15	62.3
KSU	Kansas City Southern	1/11/2019	0.86	12.9	TP15	15.7
JBHT	J.B. Hunt Transport Services, Inc.	1/18/2019	0.81	19.7	TP15	14
LUV	Southwest Airlines Company	1/18/2019	0.79	16.1	TP15	15.8
AES	The AES Corporation	1/23/2019	0.99	14.8	TP15	18.4
UTX	United Technologies Corporation	1/23/2019	0.82	14.7	TP15	18.1
CSX	CSX Corporation	2/12/2019	0.94	21	TP15	17.2
MATX	Matson, Inc.	2/25/2019	0.92	22.4	TP15	12.3

II. *Strong downtrend (recession) from 10/9/2007 to 03/09/2009, uptrend later from 03/09/2009 to 5/13/2009:*

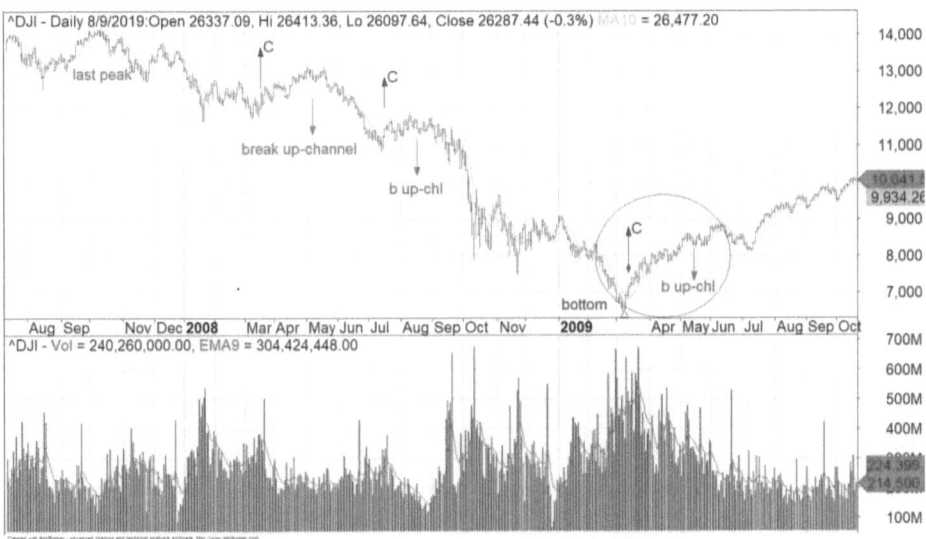

Figure 6-8: Daily chart, Dow Jones (^DJI) 2017-2019

a. Watching list:

To have the watching list in Mar 2009, the 65 stocks in three Dow Jones index groups, we can search through the Wikipedia:

i. https://en.wikipedia.org/wiki/Historical_components_of_the_Dow_Jones_Industrial_Average

ii. https://en.wikipedia.org/wiki/Dow_Jones_Transportation_Average

iii. https://en.wikipedia.org/wiki/Dow_Jones_Utility_Average

The watching list consists of 65 stocks as follows: MMM - 3M Company; AA - Alcoa Inc.; AXP - American Express Company; T - AT&T Inc.; BAC - Bank of America Corporation; BA - The Boeing Company; CAT - Caterpillar Inc.; CVX - Chevron Corporation; C -

Citigroup Inc.; KO - The Coca-Cola Company; DD - E.I. du Pont de Nemours & Company; XOM - Exxon Mobil Corporation; GE - General Electric Company; GM - General Motors Corporation; HPE - Hewlett-Packard Company; HD - The Home Depot, Inc.; INTC - Intel Corporation; IBM - International Business Machines Corporation; JNJ - Johnson & Johnson; JPM - JPMorgan Chase & Co.; KHC - Kraft Foods Inc.; MCD - McDonald's Corporation; MRK - Merck & Co., Inc.; MSFT - Microsoft Corporation; PFE - Pfizer Inc.; PG - The Procter & Gamble Company; UTX - United Technologies Corporation; VZ - Verizon Communications Inc.; WMT - Wal-Mart Stores, Inc.; DIS - The Walt Disney Company; AMR - AMR Corporation; AAL - American Airlines Group Inc.; GATX - GATX Corporation; CHRW - C.H. Robinson Worldwide, Inc.; CSX - CSX Corp.; DAL - Delta Air Lines; EXPD - Expeditors International; FDX - FedEx Corporation; JBHT - JB Hunt Transport Services, Inc.; JBLU - JetBlue Airways Corp.; KSU - Kansas City Southern; OSG - Overseas Shipholding Group; LSTR - Landstar System, Inc.; MATX - Matson, Inc.; NSC - Norfolk Southern Corp.; R - Ryder System, Inc.; LUV - Southwest Airlines, Inc.; UNP - Union Pacific Corp.; UAL - United Airlines Holdings; UPS - United Parcel Service, Inc.; AES - The AES Corporation; AEP - American Electric Power Co., Inc. ; WMB - Williams Companies.; CNP - CenterPoint Energy, Inc.; ED - Consolidated Edison, Inc.; D - Dominion Energy, Inc.; DUK - Duke Energy Corp.; EIX - Edison International; EXC - Exelon Corp.; FE - FirstEnergy Corp.; NEE - NextEra Energy Inc.; NI - NiSource, Inc.; PEG - Public Service Enterprise Group, Inc.; PCG - PG&E Corporation.; SO - Southern Company, Inc.

b. Check the general market:

❖ **Check recession of the general market:**
  ➢ From 10/9/2007 to 03/09/2009, the recession period lasted around 2 years.
  ➢ Rate of decline:
    • ^DJI: from 14,164.53 down to 6,547.05, down rate of 53%

- **^GSPC:** down rate of 56%
- **^IXIC:** down rate of 55%

⇨ **The market plunged strongly, recession period around 2 years.**

❖ **Look for uptrend market confirmation signal:**
  ➤ **03/09/2009: the bottom day.**
  ➤ **03/12/2009: confirmation day**, the third day since the bottom day, ^DJI: 7,170.06 > MA10 (6,822.35), up 9.5% higher than the bottom day, up-channel signal. Starting from that day, we can consider buying stocks.

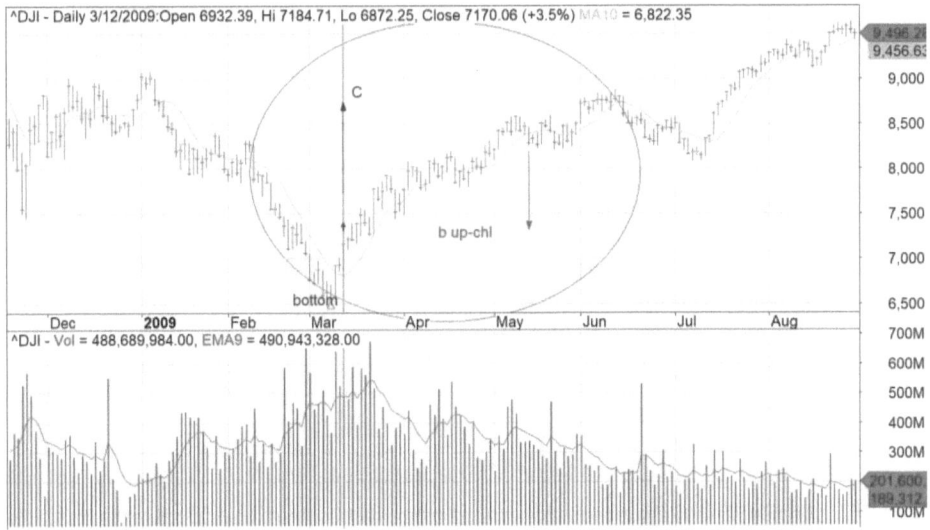

Figure 6-9: Daily chart, Dow Jones (^DJI) 2008-2009, one detail uptrend from Mar to Jun.

  ➤ Market uptrend lasted until 05/13/2009: under MA10, break up-channel. We should sell all the stocks on that day.

c. How to Buy and Sell:

❖ Use the above watching list.

❖ Find stock whose R.S >= R.S of the general market (^DJI, ^GSPC, ^IXIC), and rank them from the largest to the smallest.

✦ **On 03/12/2009, we had the list:**

- R.S of the general market at $03/12/2009$ = Max R.S (^DJI, ^GSPC, ^IXIC) = 12.4% (of ^IXIC).
- Make the filter and rank; we had the list in the below table.

Ticker	Date/Ti...	🔍1	C	%C/C-1	Vol/EMA9	B.O	Evaluate	Type	>Ma10	I.S	R.S	%🔍²	%Date-BottomMarket	Take Profit 15%	%BreakUpChannel-Confirmation
C	3/12/2009	16.70	8.4	0.8					1	0.06	59.0		63.7	TP15	104.2
JPM	3/12/2009	23.20	13.7	1.1					1	0.47	45.9		45.9	TP15	46.8
AXP	3/12/2009	13.15	10.2	1.2					1	0.26	23.6		28.2	TP15	83.2
GATX	3/12/2009	16.77	5.9	1.0					1	0.33	20.9		20.9	TP15	52.4
R	3/12/2009	23.00	-0.3	1.0					1	0.30	19.4		19.4	TP15	11.5
INTC	3/12/2009	14.52	4.0	1.0					1	0.58	15.7		18.2	TP15	4.2
MRK	3/12/2009	24.03	9.5	1.2					1	0.54	14.5		14.5	TP15	6.8
MMM	3/12/2009	48.00	2.6	0.8					1	0.58	14.1		14.8	TP15	18.6
JBHT	3/12/2009	21.19	2.8	1.2					1	0.53	14.0		14.0	TP15	21.1
CAT	3/12/2009	27.02	2.7	0.7					1	0.32	13.0		21.9	TP15	33.5
UPS	3/12/2009	43.27	1.3	0.8					1	0.58	13.0		13.0	TP15	21.1
FDX	3/12/2009	38.56	2.7	0.7					0	0.39	12.5		12.5	TP15	36.7

Figure 6-10: Ranked list on 03/12/2009 of stocks whose R.S >= R.S of the general market, the bottom day: 03/09/2009

In the table, you can see some columns:

❖ The column "Take profit 15%": All stocks list, we can take profit 15%, if we buy on the confirmation date.

❖ Column "%BreakUpChannel-Confirmation": a lot of stocks, we can get very high profit: C (104.2%), JPM (46.8%), AXP (83.2%), GATX (52.4%), R (11.5%), INTC (4.2%), MRK (6.8%), MMM (18.6%), JBHT (21.1%), CAT (33.5%), UPS (21.1%), FDX (36.7%)

❖ Some typical charts:

1. **Citigroup Inc. (C):**

Figure 6-11: Daily chart, C (Citigroup, Inc.) 2009

2. JMP Group LLC (JMP):

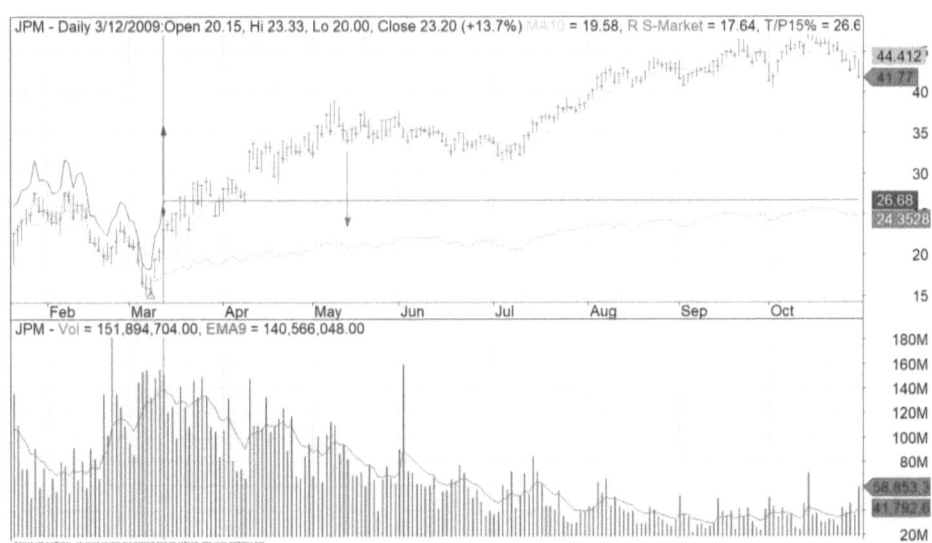

Figure 6-12: Daily chart, JMP (JMP Group LLC) 2009

3. American Express Company (AXP):

AXP - Daily 3/12/2009:Open 11.76, Hi 13.38, Lo 11.09, Close 13.15 (+10.2%) MA10 = 11.51, R.S-Market = 11.81, T/P15% = 15.1

AXP - Vol = 39,570,500.00, EMA9 = 31,680,026.00

Figure 6-13: Daily chart, AXP (American Express C.) 2009

- On the next days: From this day till 05/13/2009, we checked out the stocks' R.S of the watching list (65 stocks) belonging to the Dow Jones above every day. We considered to sell if the stocks' R.S is lower than the general market's R.S. In case the stocks' R.S maintain higher than the general market's R.S, and to be on the top; they will be successful stocks in coming time.

- In the period from 13 March 2009 to 13 May 2009, the stocks were successful (meeting the condition of taking profit 15%):

Ticker	Name	Nice Buy Date	I.S on Buy Date	R.S on Buy Date	Take Profit 15%	%BreakUpChannel-Confirmation
C	Citigroup Inc.	3/12/2009	0.06	59	TP15	104.2
JPM	J P Morgan Chase & Co	3/12/2009	0.47	45.9	TP15	46.8
AXP	American Express Company	3/12/2009	0.26	23.6	TP15	83.2
GATX	GATX Corporation	3/12/2009	0.33	20.9	TP15	52.4
R	Ryder System, Inc.	3/12/2009	0.3	19.4	TP15	11.5
INTC	Intel Corporation	3/12/2009	0.58	15.7	TP15	4.2
MRK	Merck & Company, Inc.	3/12/2009	0.54	14.5	TP15	6.8
MMM	3M Company	3/12/2009	0.58	14.1	TP15	18.6
JBHT	J.B. Hunt Transport Services, Inc.	3/12/2009	0.53	14	TP15	21.1
CAT	Caterpillar, Inc.	3/12/2009	0.32	13	TP15	33.5
UPS	United Parcel Service, Inc.	3/12/2009	0.58	13	TP15	21.1
FDX	FedEx Corporation	3/12/2009	0.39	12.5	TP15	36.7
EIX	Edison International	3/13/2009	0.51	15.9	TP15	9.5
HD	Home Depot, Inc. (The)	3/13/2009	0.69	13.6	TP15	22.1
LSTR	Landstar System, Inc.	3/16/2009	0.55	16.8	TP15	15.7
UNP	Union Pacific Corporation	3/16/2009	0.46	15.8	TP15	23.3
CHRW	C.H. Robinson Worldwide, Inc.	3/16/2009	0.65	15.7	TP15	18.3
NSC	Norfolk Souther Corporation	3/16/2009	0.42	15.2	TP15	16.8
EXPD	Expeditors International of Washington, Inc.	3/16/2009	0.56	13.9	TP15	22.8
AA	Alcoa Corporation	3/16/2009	0.14	13.5	TP15	44.3
NEE	NextEra Energy, Inc.	3/16/2009	0.68	11.7	TP15	24.6
DUK	Duke Energy Corporation	3/18/2009	0.74	18.5	TP15	11
ED	Consolidated Edison Inc	3/20/2009	0.82	15.6	TP15	1.6
PEG	Public Service Enterprise Group Incorporated	3/24/2009	0.62	20.1	TP15	32.3
DD	DuPont de Nemours, Inc.	3/26/2009	0.22	48	TP15	122.6
MSFT	Microsoft Corporation	3/31/2009	0.58	21.3	TP15	16.1
DIS	Walt Disney Company (The)	4/2/2009	0.58	29.6	TP15	35.4
MATX	Matson, Inc.	4/29/2009	0.53	67.5	TP15	19.8
BA	Boeing Company (The)	5/5/2009	0.5	39.2	TP15	27.7
GE	General Electric Company	5/6/2009	0.42	84.5	TP15	34.9
UTX	United Technologies Corporation	5/6/2009	0.7	39.2	TP15	21.1
BAC	Bank of America Corporation	5/7/2009	0.35	260.3	TP15	88.2
WMB	Williams Companies, Inc. (The)	5/8/2009	0.4	61.6	TP15	33.1

Chapter 7: STRATEGY 2 - BUY AND MANAGE BEST GROWTH STOCKS IN TEN MINUTES

✓ *Necessary condition: Leading growth stocks in an uptrend general market.*
✓ *Sufficient condition: Fundamental analysis is good enough (stable business results and speeds up recently).*

The growth investment strategy is the classic investment strategy of all famous growth investors in the world. However, the author presents in a bit different angle, and the criteria are also a little different while patterns are as same as the other books' one. The given criteria are easy to quantify, help all investors to reach the exceptional and quality result, no matter they have experience in the market or not.

The steps quantify 100% of the criteria, are easy to implement and evaluate.

The backtest to verify the method is also simple, correct, and effective. The readers don't need to worry about repainting from signs on buying and selling stocks.

You can double-check your selection results with the information provided by growth investment advisors around the world, which will give similar results.

Why is this method safe and effective?

During an uptrend, a group of stocks that are stronger than the general market (by R.S checking) shall pull the market up. These stocks keep on rising to save the general market up. After that, the general market pulls the other stocks up. If the market is an uptrend, there will be a certain number of stocks that reach the target price (the price will increase by 20-25% higher than the appropriate point of purchase).

The stocks have satisfactory fundamental analysis results as the business is stable and grows for the last three years, revenue and earning speed up recently. These stocks are going to increase in the coming period.

Choosing the correct ones, the probability of success is 70-80%.

1. Model activities of a successful growth stock:

In the long term, stock development consists of two stages: a base stage and a growth stage.

❖ A base stage: maybe lasting for a few weeks to several years. In this period, stock works within the range of investors' mindset price. At the appropriate opportunity (the company shows good business results, or appears a special event, in the context of an uptrend general market). Stock prices will jump to a new stage.

❖ A growth stage: stock price increase is considerable, usually 20-40% in the period of a few weeks to a few months.

Learning the characteristics of growth stage to see there are many rules, and repetitive characteristics, that shall establish the steps to improve effective trading methods and minimize risk.

Buying stocks in the growth stage will help investors have the best investment efficiency without capital backlog or waiting time.

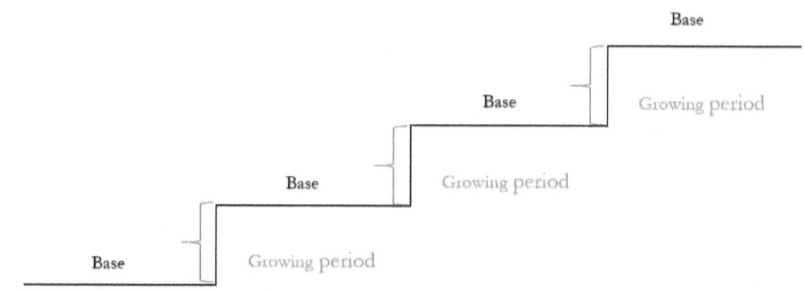

Figure 7-1: Stock growing, including many base stages, many growth stages

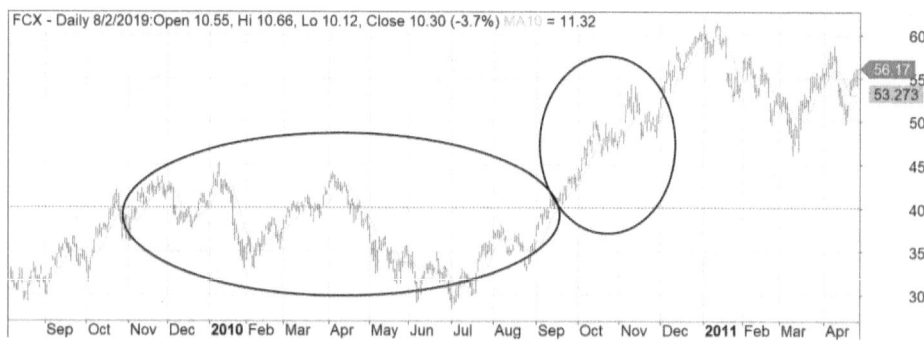

Figure 7-2: Daily chart, FCX, Aug09-Aug10: base creating, Sep10-Dec10: growth period

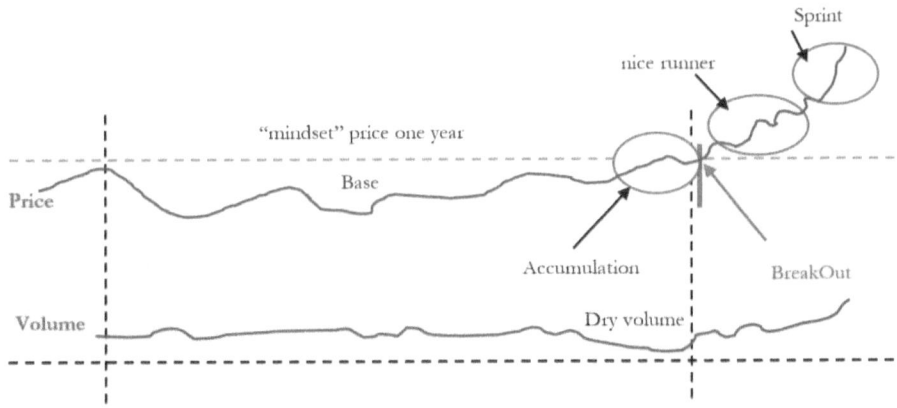

Figure 7-3: Typical stock activities at growth period

- ❖ **Base**: The price of a stock fluctuates within a narrow range for a specific period. In its development, each stock can go through many bases (the price gap is 20-40% between bases)
- ❖ **Accumulation**: In one base, the stock price fluctuates in a very narrow range; investors trade with a small and stable volume, which means they are collecting gently, and no one has divested strongly.
- ❖ **Breakout point** (boom point): Stock is bought in massive quantities; price rises sharply.
- ❖ **The stock runs reasonably (nice runner)**: after a breakout, Stock maintains "up-channel" reasonably.
- ❖ **Sprint**: Continuous increase for 3-4 days, the total increase is by 10-20% (almost no adjustment)
- ❖ **"Mindset" price**: The price where most investors agree to keep for a specified period (higher price: to be sold, lower price: to be bought). "Mindset" price is different from Resistance (ceiling limit) or Support (floor limit) level in the short term.

Figure 7-4: One-year mindset price (AMZN: Jul2018-Jul2019)

The highest mindset price of "baby" periods is considered to be the mindset price of an extended period (usually one year).

In this chart, the AMZN mindset price from Jul2018-Jul2019 = 1.970$ (green dashed long line).

2. Insurance and balance account protection:

a. *Stop Loss at -7%, Take Profit at 20%*

For both the value investment method, or the growth investment method, there is no way to correctly choose 100% of the stock that works as you expected in your investment strategy. Even the most seasoned investors cannot be sure of picking stocks, some stocks in the portfolio help them to win big, and some cannot help them make money or even get lost. However, over time, the value of the wins is enough to compensate for the loss, the investors can survive and get rich. It is understood that choosing successful stocks is a probability; buying a take-profit stock is also a probability, although the rules and criteria of the investment strategy remain unchanged.

For growth investment strategy, early detection of wrong stock choice is even more critical. When a mistake is discovered, growth investors need to stop. Continuing to hold unwanted stocks makes you become a blind investor, and will suffer heavy losses.

There are many unexpected scripts that may happen to enterprises, including macro to micro factors, such as the board of directors, business strategy, business operations, partners, opponents, politics, war, media crisis; all of them can affect business circumstances. If you insist on putting our faith in enterprise blindly, you will turn into a reluctant value investor.

We are looking in the past, during the period of prolonged crisis such as July 2007 - Sep 2009, Mar 2000 – Jan 2003, 1987-1988, 1980-1982. If you had not admitted the mistake and run away from the market, inevitably you would be severely affected and subjected to severe devastation of your accounts. Alternatively, if you borrow money from the broker company, you would take the risk of burning the whole balanced account.

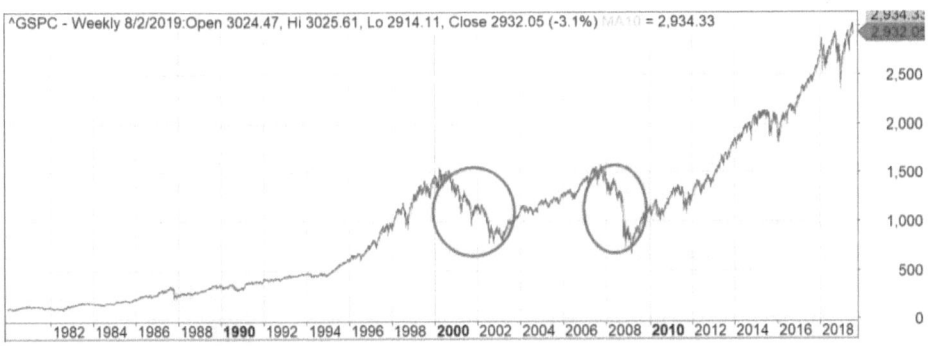

Figure 7-5: S&P500 (^GSPC), weekly, 1982-2019

For example, some stocks get down such as:

- ➢ S from 70 (Y2000) - 10 (Y2002) - 3 (Y2009).
- ➢ TEF: 34 (Y2008) - 8 (Y2019), ….

Imaging of holding one of these stocks, the results will be devastating.

Figure 7-6: Sprint Corporation (S), weekly, 2000-2009

Figure 7-7: Telefónica, S.A. (TEF), 2008-2019

On the other hand, when you hold a decreasing stock, you will feel tired and lousy. It always seems to dominate your mind and affect all other activities. Trading will no longer be alert and lucid. Therefore, when you find yourself wrong, you need to eliminate the mistake as soon as possible.

Predicting the bottom of the stock is also a dangerous action, like trying to catch a falling knife. We cannot know for sure whether we will grasp the grip or the blade. The probability of success is very low, but the chance of being wounded is very high.

Another reason is that insistence on holding a losing stock means you miss the opportunity to buy another winning stock.

In summary, being conservative in not liquidating, cutting losses is very hazardous and will burn the account, miss the opportunity, and lose capital.

The author evaluates the loss ratio (loss), and the profit ratio (profit to get even) as below:

Loss (%)	Profit to get even
-5%	+5.3%
-7%	+7.5%
-10%	+11.1%
-20%	+25.0%
-33%	+50.0%
-50%	+100.0%

Accepting a high stop-loss rate means finding a high-profit rate to compensate for losses. However, finding a stock that brings high profit is very difficult, and requires a very long time (profit level of 50% or more rarely appears). Thus, it would be best if you built a reasonable level of stop-loss, ensuring the compensate opportunity at the highest. The recommended maximum loss level is not bigger than 10%.

A good buying order requires the detail of stop loss value (SL), and take profit value (TP) in advance.

The stock moves like a ball bouncing between two lines: TP, SL, and you can let the stock move until it touches to the TP or SL line.

Figure 7-8: Model of stock oscillation between TP and SL edge

The SL is too low if it is around 3% or 5%. The SL order has the risk of being closed before there is a chance to bounce again to win. The SL should be around 7-10%.

When learning the characteristics of successful growth stocks, the author found that the adjustment level usually does not exceed 7% in the growth stage. The price increase is generally by 20-30% to the next higher base.

Therefore, for safe transactions, the author advises choosing TP: 20%, SL: -7% (TP / SL corresponds to the 3/1 ratio). That is the optimal ratio. In this game, among three transactions of the same value, if one wins, two lose at the above rate, we still gain a 6% profit.

The purpose of the game is to survive in the market, and the more you play, the more advantage you get. Giving the safe ratio the SL at -7%, and the TP at 20%. Controlling to reach a 60% winning transaction of the total is the goal of this "game."

b. Only buy stocks in uptrend general market

70% of stocks follow the market trend. The uptrend, 70% of stocks go up; on the contrary, downtrend, 70% of stocks go down.

First, the general market score is the average of stocks, so they reflect and go up or go down together with stocks.

Second, psychological consensus. Many stocks increased to lead the general market to be up. The uptrend market pulls many stocks following its' trend. It is the same in the case of a downward direction.

The indexes having a strong influence on stock movement are the following: Dow Jones Industrial Average (^ DJI), S&P 500 (^ GSPC), NASDAQ Composite (^IXIC).

Therefore, you, the growth investors should find the best point to maximize the chance of increasing and minimize the risk of devaluation. You only participate in the period of clearly uptrend market. In a downtrend or a sideway, you had better wait patiently and keep your cash.

You might have heard some legendary growth investors saying: "I do not buy stocks, I buy the general market, stocks are only the object I disburse." That shows the importance of following the market trend to buy stocks.

Following the trend of the general market, you have more opportunities to win, increase the probability of success, and bring profit when buying or holding stocks.

3. Identify market trends:

a. *How to identify market trends?*

Identify the market trend is to assess the general market **at present** and determine the trend is now going up or down, and it is suitable to buy, hold, or sell stocks.

Determining the general market trend is not judging or forecasting how the market will be in 3 months, 9 months, 12 months; or when the market goes up or down; or how much the Dow Jones Industrial Average (^ DJI), S&P 500 (^ GSPC), or NASDAQ Composite (^ IXIC) is in the future. No one can do that unless you are a great prophet. That approaching way is wrong, and a lack of scientific basis.

The movement of the market is reflecting the buying demand, the selling demand of investors, especially big ones. Based on this characteristic, we can identify the market trend scientifically and effectively.

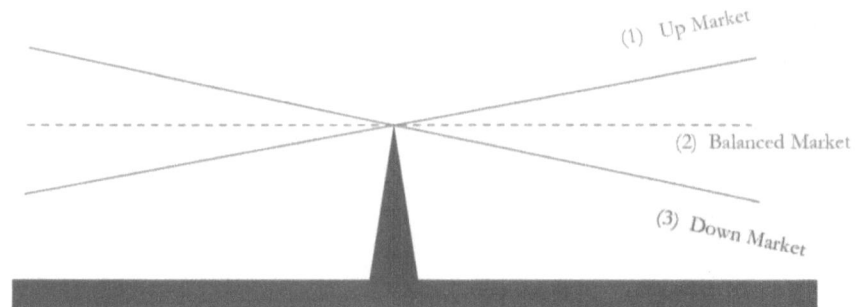

Figure 7-9: Model of balanced Market

The chart above reflects the market equilibrium level, supply/demand balance, and market deviation on uptrend or downtrend.

❖ Case (1): Market is uptrend. The number of investors who expect the market to go up is more. Cashflow or the amount of buying is more than selling. Cashflow shows greed.

❖ Case (2): The market is balanced; supply/ demand is balanced; the cashflow to buy is equal to the cashflow to sell. The market does not show greed or fear. The market is flat.

❖ Case (3): Market is downtrend. The number of investors taking profit is high; selling is more than buying. Cashflow shows fear.

Identifying the general market trend is to check out the current market is uptrend or downtrend, in the direction of buying, or selling. If the market unbalanced forward the buying direction, it would be safe to buy and hold stocks. If the market is in the course of selling, it is better to be far away from the market, holding cash.

Through the critical market indexes, including Dow Jones Industrial Average (^ DJI), S&P 500 (^ GSPC), NASDAQ Composite (^ IXIC), and the activities of market-leading stocks in each wave, we can fully assess the current situation of the general market to make decisions: "Buy", "Just hold", "Sell out".

We don't need to use any other indicators; all we need is just information about the general market (key market indexes, volume), and top leading stocks (price and volume). This primary information, along with the scientific analysis method, will help us determine exactly the general market trends.

b. Signals to confirm the general market trend:

Learned from the characteristics of the market in history, we will choose the periods of uptrend, stability, unbalanced market in the upward direction, to enter the market:

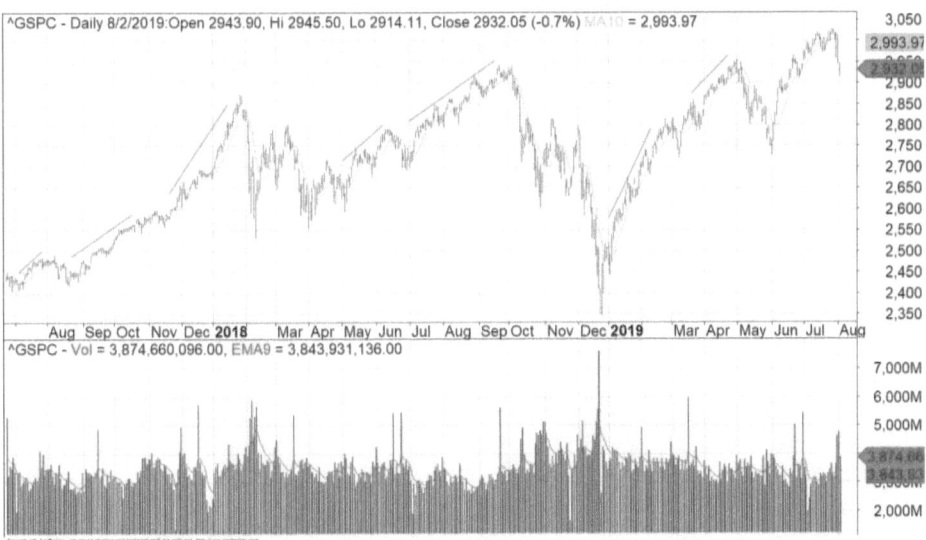

Figure 7-10: S&P500 (^GSPC) & Moving Average 10 days (SMA10), Jul2017-Jul2019

We must remember that we cannot make money in all situations of the general market. Being wise is to choose the most advantageous chance in the uptrend market period to join. Remember: "Losing money by ourselves, earning money is due to the market," this is a saying that growth investors must never forget. Therefore, we must always pay attention first: "general market, general market, general market." The figure above shows some advantage periods expressed by go-up diagonal lines, which are safe, stable, growing, and favorable. These periods bring great opportunities to buy and hold stocks.

❖ *Signal of Simple Moving Average 10 days (MA10):*

If the market is down, the general market score - EOD value would usually be under the MA10 line, everything is in a rush to be sold out. If the market is up, stable, and safe, the general market score often follows and stays above the MA10 line. You can look at Figure 7-10,11,12 to see the characteristics of the market.

Therefore, we can use MA10 as a criterion to observe, evaluate whether the market is in an uptrend or not. A few of the examples below will help to be more transparent:

Figure 7-11: NASDAQ (^IXIC) & Moving Average 10 days (SMA10), Jul2018-Jul2019

Figure 7-12: Dow Jones (^DJI) & Moving Average 10 days (SMA10), May2017-Apr2018

❖ *Signal of up-channel, down-channel:*

What is up-channel or down-channel? Let us imagine a pile of sand left outside, after a while, affected by rain and wind. Around the sandpile, the surface will be formed curves from top to bottom. Looking at that surface, that is easy to associate and explain the up-channel and down-channel.

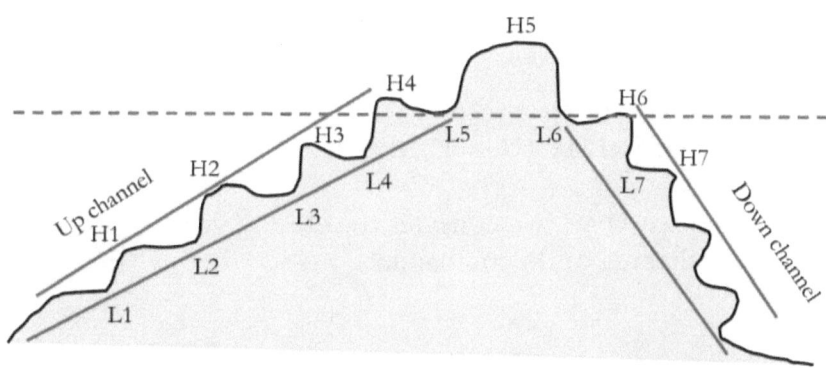

Figure 7-13: Image of up-channel and down-channel

Explanation: L: Low, H: High.

Up-channel: The line is going up

67

with: L1 < L2 < L3 < L4 < L5

H1 < H2 < H3 < H4 < H5

Down-channel: The line is going down

with: L5 > L6 > L7 > ...

H5 > H6 > H7 > ...

"Low" and "High" are named as support value and resistant value in the "mindset" of investors.

"Low" value is the negative status of investors. "High" value is their positive status.

In the up-channel: The level of "mindset" of Low, and High are increasing. Vice versa, in the down-channel: The "mindset" of Low, and High are decreasing.

Some examples of the up-channel, down-channel market:

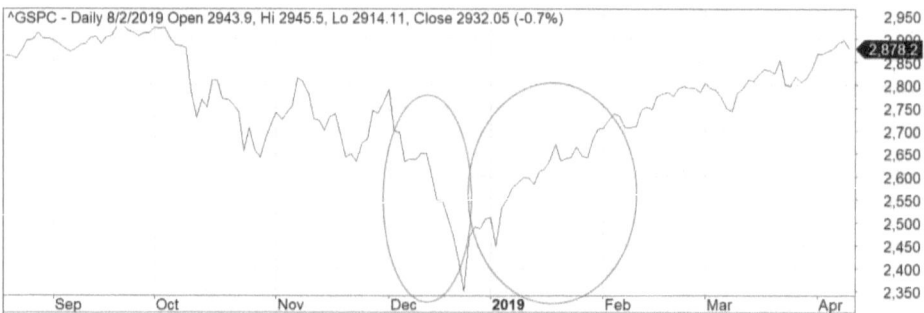

Figure 7-14: S&P500 (^GSPC), down-channel, up-channel

When using a bar chart, we consider the closing value of the day to confirm the up-channel or down-channel.

Figure 7-15: Nasdaq (^IXIC), daily, EOD, up-channel

❖ *Uptrend market confirmation day:*

When the general market goes down, we are out of the market. In order to start jumping into the market, we need to find the nearest "bottom day" and the uptrend market confirmation day. The uptrend market confirmation day is compulsory to satisfy two criteria: cross higher than the MA10 line, and start creating a new upward direction.

The market goes up; the trend does not take place in 1 or 2 days, or 1 or 2 weeks. It usually lasts for weeks, even months. So, we do not need to buy stocks randomly and hurriedly. Firstly, we need to find a clear bottom day, then we ignore some days, even for one week, waiting for the day that the general market index to pass the MA10 line, show a clear signal of up-channel, and R.S of general index reaches 2.5% higher than the bottom day.

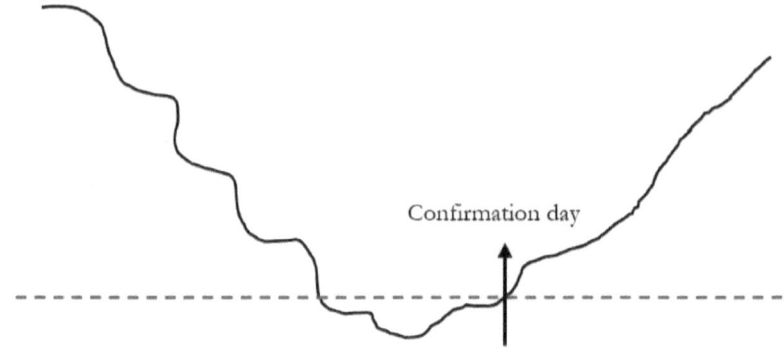

Figure 7-16: Confirmation day

Figure 7-17: Nasdaq (^IXIC), daily, confirmation day

Upon the confirmation day, we start to choose the best stock to buy.

❖ *Date of breaking the up-channel:*

The date of breaking up-channel is understood as the day that the signal of up-channel is lost. It does not mean that the market is certain to fall, but it is possible depending on the level of market equilibrium which is broken, the level of negative "mindset" price of investors who violate the principle. Therefore, there is a sign of danger.

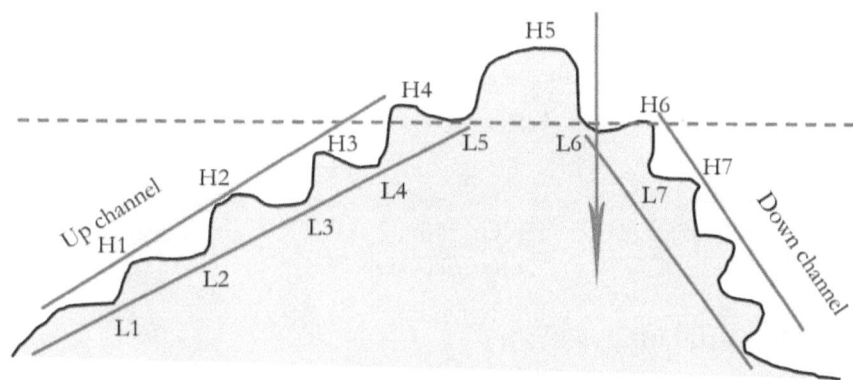

Figure 7-18: Date of the breaking of up-channel

During the uptrend, indexes under the MA10 line are also dangerous, and highly risky of a downtrend. Alternatively, even if the market has not gone down yet, the stock price volatility is enormous. We need to pay close attention to the first days under the MA10 line until the general market confirms uptrend and higher than the MA10 line again.

In short, on the date of breaking the up-channel, and indexes are also under the MA10 line, this is a very risk day. Since this date appears, we consider selling all stocks, except the stocks are in "green" color or "sprinting," or holding profit more than 10%. However, we must monitor stocks closely to liquidate as soon as possible, if needed.

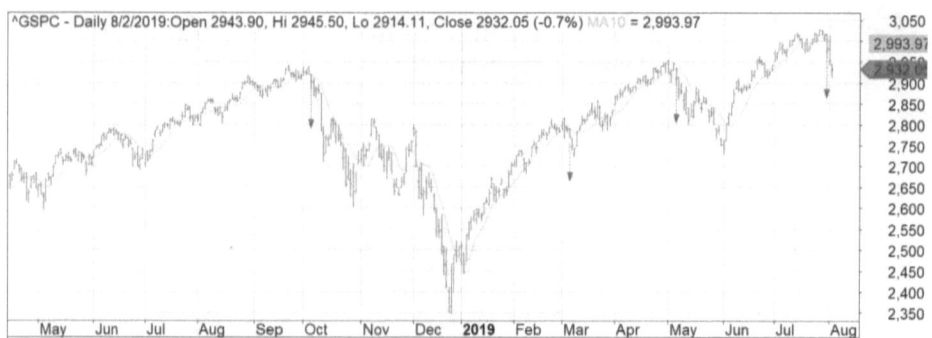

Figure 7-19: S&P500 (^GSPC) daily, 2018-2019, and breaking up-channel day

4. Fundamental analysis

According to traditional growth investors, fundamental analysis will be carried out first to create the watching list, even before analyzing the general market. Technical analysis will be conducted later to find suitable buying points and selling points.

In the author's view, the technical analysis shall be conducted in advance to assess opportunities and the ability to succeed. After that, fundamental analysis will be performed under the purpose of checking the "sufficient" conditions, because enterprises need to be confirmed about operation quality, and current business results.

To make it easier for the readers, in this chapter, the content of fundamental analysis was given before the content of the technical analysis.

a. *Fundamental analysis:*

❖ *Why need to make fundamental analysis:*

Enterprise foundation, business results play an essential role in increasing the stock price.

If the reason to increase the stock price is because of business results, the increase will be stable and sustainable, and the growth level will be enough to bring investors profit as their expectation (20-40 %).

Buying stocks with good fundamental analysis results shall limit the risk (especially the risk of failing/bankruptcy).

Stocks with good fundamental analysis results are likely owned by huge investment funds, institutions, and board of management of the company.

❖ *Stock and company :*

In the long term, the growth rate of enterprises is proportional to the level increase of its stock price (opportunity for value investors to gamble), the smart investment funds will very soon discover and want to own such businesses.

However, in the short term, enterprises and stock prices are not like that. If the transaction is "short-term" (less than a few years), it is impossible to consider these two objects as one.

Therefore, fundamental analysis is only a "sufficient" condition for deciding to trade. For each quarter, there was only one financial report; meanwhile, the stock price could increase from 2 to 4 times in that period.

❖ *Transparency financial statements in Fundamental analysis:*

If you think the financial statements may not be transparent, or not clear enough, you had better see the most transparent, simplest parts of the report.

Focusing on analyzing the following factors: Revenue, Earnings, EPS, ROE. They are the most simple, accurate, and difficult to distort indicators.

❖ *80/20 principle, and Glacier principle in Fundamental analysis:*

80/20 Principle: That is, 80% of the factors affect only 20% of the price increase, while 20% of other key factors affect 80% of the work.

Glacier principle: That is, we only see the tip of the iceberg, while we cannot see 80-90% of the sank.

❖ *Analyzing the present, not predicting the future:*

For example, you are an employee in the XYZ company, or you are the owner of the company. I ask you one question, can you evaluate your company's business results in the next year, the next two years and next three years? Maybe, but how it is exact? 40% -50% -60%.

For companies known only through the internet, do you need to read about their prospects in the next few years?

My advice for you: Read and understand "current" things about the business. Do not predict the future. A company with three years of stable and sustainable growth, strong growth in the latest quarter will undoubtedly be safer than a currently tragic business but planning a very bright prospect.

b. Guideline for Fundamental analysis:

❖ *The principle:*

Only analyze Revenue, Earnings, EPS, ROE indicators, and only analyze "the current," do not predict the future.

Fundamental analysis is just the "sufficient" condition for stock rising. The "necessary" condition is the buying demand from huge investment funds, institutions funds. The stock price is reflected in the level of supply/ demand of all investors.

Stocks must be placed in the same frame, the same checklist when analyzing; do not love, hate, bias, prejudice against any stock. If you are an expert in banking, then do not "love" or analyze more information when making fundamental analysis on a bank.

❖ *Stable growth enterprises, high ROE for the long-term:*

Growth in the last three years: Are Revenue, Earnings, EPS stable increasing by 15%? Is the annual ROE of the latest three years higher than 15%?

Purpose: Looking for stable and sustainable growth for three years. Three-year information gave specified numbers, proving that enterprises have partly passed the natural selection, and have the opportunity to accelerate and breakout later.

❖ *Recent sudden growth:*

Recent sudden growth: the enterprise's income increases very fast recently.

We need to make a comparison: quarter Revenue, quarter Earnings vs. the same periods last year, and the YTQ (year to quarter) of this year vs. the YTQ of the previous year. The increasing should be higher than 25%; but in some cases, 15% is acceptable.

Sudden growth business demonstrates that companies have big changed about: products, production, technology innovation, customer, or better cost management, etc.

Meaning: Looking for possibilities that stock price may breakout and increase considerably.

❖ *Supporting information:*

In some cases, good news or bad news does not affect stock price movement; except terrible news, the stock price will plunge suddenly.

New information includes new products, new leadership, new technologies, even buying and selling action of some institutional funds, etc.

If that news comes out, the stocks can make a price breakout point, run well later, the news is surely "good" and supports well to price movement.

c. Collect data to make fundamental analysis:

i. The data source used:

https://finance.yahoo.com, https://www.nasdaq.com, https://www.marketwatch.com are quite reliable statistic pages about stock and business data (Using statistical information, not "judgment and forecast" information).

You copy or download data to use.

ii. Fundamental analysis forms:

❖ *Stable growth business for the latest three years:*
➤ Analyzing the business results in the latest three years
➤ Answer two questions:
  - Annual growth in Revenue, Net income, EPS is increasing by 15%? In some cases, increasing by 5-10% is acceptable.
  - ROE is more than 15%? In some industries, more than 10% is acceptable.
  - Example:

Items	2016	2017	2018	2018 vs 2017	2017 vs 2016	Answer the question	Good, OK, Not
Revenue	r3	r2	r1	r1/r2	r2/r3		
Net income	ni3	ni2	ni1	ni1/ni2	ni2/ni3	Every year, increased %? 15%, 10%, 5%	
EPS	e3	e2	e1	e1/e2	e2/e3		
ROE	roe3	roe2	roe1			ROE >= %? 15%, 10%	

Analysis time: Aug.2019

❖ *Sudden growth business recently:*
➤ Analyzing the business results in the last quarter. Compare the last quarter vs. the same period last year, and compare the YTQ

(year to quarter) of this year vs. the same YTQ of the previous year.

➢ Answer one questions:

- Quarter and YTQ earnings growth in Revenue, Net income, EPS are increasing by 25%? In some cases, increasing by 10-15% is acceptable.

- Example:

Items	Q1. 18	Q2. 18	Q3. 18	Q4. 18	Q1. 19	Q2. 19	Q2.19 vs Q2.18	YTQ.19 vs YTQ.18	Answer the question	Good, OK, Not
Revenue	r15	r14	r13	r12	r11	r10	r10/ r14	(r10+r11) / (r14+r15)	Same period, same YTQ increased%? 25%, 15%, 10%	
Net income	ni15	ni14	ni13	ni12	ni11	ni10	ni10/ ni14	(ni10+ni11)/ (ni14+ni15)		
EPS	e15	e14	e13	e12	e11	e10	e10/ e14	(e10+e11) / (e14+e15)		

Analysis time: Aug.2019

❖ *Supported, additional information:*

➢ Business information and stock movement of sibling companies in the same industry group.

➢ New product, new technology, new leadership.

➢ News of buying, selling, and acquisition.

These kinds of information may affect the stock price movement.

❖ *Conclusion:*

To buy stocks, we need to do fundamental analyzing. We only buy the enterprise that has stable growth business in the latest three years, high ROE, fast-growth earnings recently, and is supported by some good news.

It is not true that the higher the fundamental analysis score is, the better the chances of the growing price will be. Fundamental analysis is only one condition (sufficient condition), ensuring the enterprises are safe, stable growth, and have factors to accelerate stock price. If the fundamental analysis score of stock meets 80% of the above principle, it will be considered to pass the fundamental analysis.

5. How to buy:

In the uptrend market period after a recession, we buy blue-chip stocks that were owned by significant investment funds. While, in an uptrend period of a growth market, we trade on the growth stocks. They are often the stocks of smaller capitalization companies, unknown, but their price increase sharply, because of their outstanding products, or technology. These companies are likely healthy boys who are growing up into strong men.

We apply both technical analysis and fundamental analysis to buy growth stocks. Technical analysis is the first step to filter the list of stocks that meet the technical analysis specification; fundamental analysis is the next to confirm whether the stocks are safe and have outstanding factors or not.

Technical analysis helps us to utilize "successful stock models," find the optimal buying points, where the chance of price increase is the highest, the risk of decreasing is the smallest. It also helps us see the "smart money" and "nice stories" behind the breakout point of stock. The technical analysis finds out stocks whose R.S higher than the general market's R.S. The high R.S stocks will be able to continue rising, leading, and supporting the general market up. Technical analysis is a necessary condition.

The fundamental analysis shall qualify stocks to ensure they comply with some requirements: stable growth business, high ROE, earning speed up recently. Fundamental analysis is the sufficient condition.

How to buy growth stocks for the most optimal profit and the smallest risk? Let's review the model of successful growth stocks (Chapter 7, item No. 1) to know the way of building clear criteria and the method of buying quantitatively and scientifically.

The technical analysis's criteria to select stocks are as follows (daily chart)

❖ **Breakout stock:** Stock is bought strongly, price rises sharply, and the trading volume becomes large. At this time, big investors accepted to reveal their trading volume, clearly showed the demand for holding stocks. Investors accept to buy at a high price, together agree that the stock deserves a higher price. Breakout stock signals are often as following: Price increases at least 2% compared to the closing price of the previous day; trading volume increases at least 150% compared to the average of nine consecutive days recently.

❖ **Stocks surpassed the "one-year mindset" price**: The day that price can exceed the one-year mindset price is usually a strong breakout day. Many growth investors called "pivot point," this day shows the highest level of consensus on buying and pushing up stock prices, promoting stocks to a new price stage, surpassing the "mindset," and the expectations of investors during the past one year. This day will usually be the optimal buying day.

AAPL - Daily 8/2/2019:Open 205.53, Hi 206.43, Lo 201.63, Close 204.02 (-2.1%) MA10 = 208.34

base, mindset 1 year

breakout, buy point

May Jun Jul Aug Sep Oct Nov Dec 2014 Feb Mar Apr May Jun Jul Aug Sep Oct

AAPL - Vol = 38,688,200.00, EMA9 = 36,225,636.00

high volume

Figure 7-20: Apple (APPL) daily, 2013-2014, mindset and buying point

- ❖ **I.S is equal to or higher than 85%:** The intrinsic strength (I.S) should be higher than 85% to prevent us from buying recovery stocks instead of growth stocks.
- ❖ **The stock's R.S is higher than the general market's R.S:** Growth stocks must go up stronger than the general market does since the nearest market bottom day. These stocks must be an excellent contribution to the rising of the market, not a burden. Therefore, R.S of stocks must be higher than R.S of the general market index since the nearest market bottom date.
- ❖ **Price is higher than the MA10 line:** That means the stock is a bull. We need the stocks whose price is above the MA10 line to avoid buying ones that are about to be weak, notably weaker than the average activity in the recent two weeks (10 trading days).
- ❖ **Buy at the first breakout point after surpassing the one-year mindset price:** Each stage of a growth stock, has an optimal buying day - the best buy point, it is the day that surpasses the one-year mindset price. After that, the active stocks will breakout

continuously. We should buy at this first breakout, to optimize profitability, and limit the risk in case the price is adjusted.

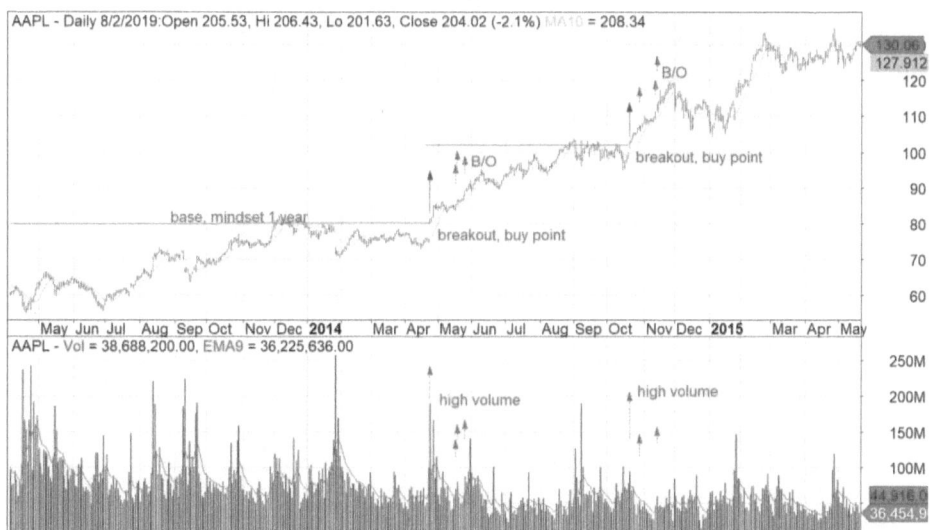

Figure 7-21: Apple (APPL) daily, 2013-2015, breakout and buy point

In case we cannot catch up to the optimal buy point, or have not enough insurance at the time, we can participate in the following trading days. However, the expected profit can decrease because the take-profit price is grounded from the optimal buy point. The higher the price you buy, the lower the profit you get. And the risk of stop-loss increases, because buying at a higher price, the ratio TP/SL is not equal to 3/1.

After finding a list of stocks that meet the buying conditions in terms of technical analysis, we check out if the company is qualified for fundamental analysis conditions (according to item No. 4 of this chapter). Some detail conditions:

➢ Stable growth business in the latest three years.
➢ Sudden growth earning recently.
➢ Additional supporting information (not compulsory).

The last thing, if there are too many stocks that meet the above buying criteria. We put the priority according to the section, or the industry in which many stocks meet the criteria. Because, typically, stocks will boom in section groups and industry groups. In a group, we put the priority on the highest R.S's stocks. That will be the leaders of the market, section, or industry later.

❖ *How to do:*
  ➢ *Find all breakout stocks on the consideration day.*
  ➢ *Draw the one-year mindset price for the current base*
  ➢ *Calculate and check I.S >= 85%, R.S of stocks >= R.S of (^DJI, ^GSPC, ^IXIC), Price >= MA10.*
  ➢ *Find the "Pivot point" or "Buy point" (first breakout that surpasses the one-year mindset price of that base).*
  ➢ *Check Fundamental analysis.*
  ➢ *Make a list, and sort by section and industry (group), then sort by R.S*
  ➢ *Choose the best players at a group that has plenty of members.*

The author recommends using Amibroker software to analyze data conveniently and quickly. Through a few code lines in the file with *.afl extension, and Amibroker's Explore tool, you can get the entire stock list no more than 2 minutes.

That's why the author named the chapter: BUY AND MANAGE BEST GROWTH STOCKS IN TEN MINUTES.

6. How to Sell:

On buying, we use both technical analysis and fundamental analysis to choose stocks and their buying points; on selling, we only use technical analysis to make the decision.

Similar to strategy No.1, we have four selling scenarios as follows.

❖ **Sell to take profit:** Reviewing historical data of growth stocks, as well as successful growth stock models, that the price moves from one base to the next; stock price can rise by 20-40%. Therefore, we choose 20% as a level to take the profit.

❖ **Sell to cut loss:** According to the TP / SL ~ ratio of 3/1, the successful growth stocks rarely decrease by 7%, and if they drop by 7%, they often fail. Therefore, the author proposes to cut loss if the price is 7% lower than the price at the up-channel confirmation day or optimal buy price. Choose the higher value.

❖ **Liquidation:** There are 2 cases in which we consider liquidating stocks, and exit the market, or find opportunities from other stocks:
  ➤ The general market: indexes break the up-channel, and under the MA10 line. The risk is from the general market trend.
  ➤ Stock's R.S is lower than the general market's R.S. The stock is not strong and supporting to the general market to grow up anymore. We should not keep laggard stocks, although they were active before.

❖ **Emergency selling:** If the stock suddenly drops by 10% or more during the trading session, we will apply the emergency method by automatic orders from the system, or through the brokers. The purpose is to cope with unexpected situations and avoid unfortunate damage.

7. Some examples in the real market (testing):

For strategy No. 1, we follow the portfolio of significant investment funds after the recession, and the general market has the signals to confirm of recovering.

For strategy No. 2 - Investment growth, we buy in almost all stages of the growth market, at the increasing time after appearing the confirmation day.

To be better to understand strategy No. 2, we select some market periods during the latest three years to prove that. We can choose any market period, but it will be best if choosing the latest period to see how the strategy is effective and how the accessing of fundamental analysis is convenient.

When evaluating the overall market, we will simultaneously consider the indicators ^ DJI, ^ GSPC, ^ IXIC.

The drawing below is the chart of ^ DJI. We mark "buying confirmation" points and "selling confirmation" points according to the general market movement (up arrow: the points to consider buying; down arrow: the point to consider selling or liquidating stocks). We take the example of analyzing to buy and sell stocks in the following two segments of the market below:

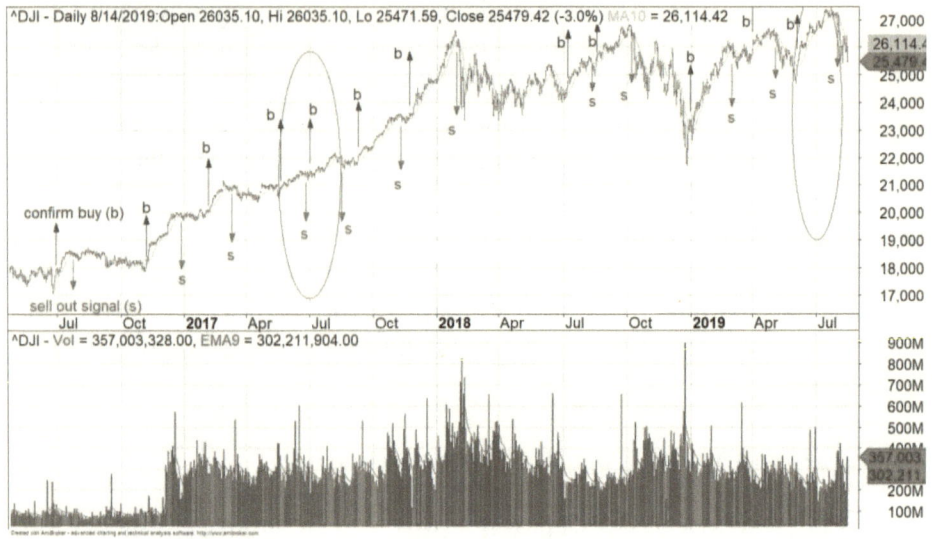

Figure 7-22: Dow Jones (^DJI) daily, 2016-2019, buying and selling confirmation day

In cases of consideration of buying/selling stocks in below, the author does not go into fundamental analysis to make sure the book is short and avoid rambling. Fundamental analysis is presented in detail in chapter 7, item No. 4, and not difficult for you to understand the content.

I. *Uptrend period from 05/17/2017 to 08/07/2017:*

a. *Check the general market*

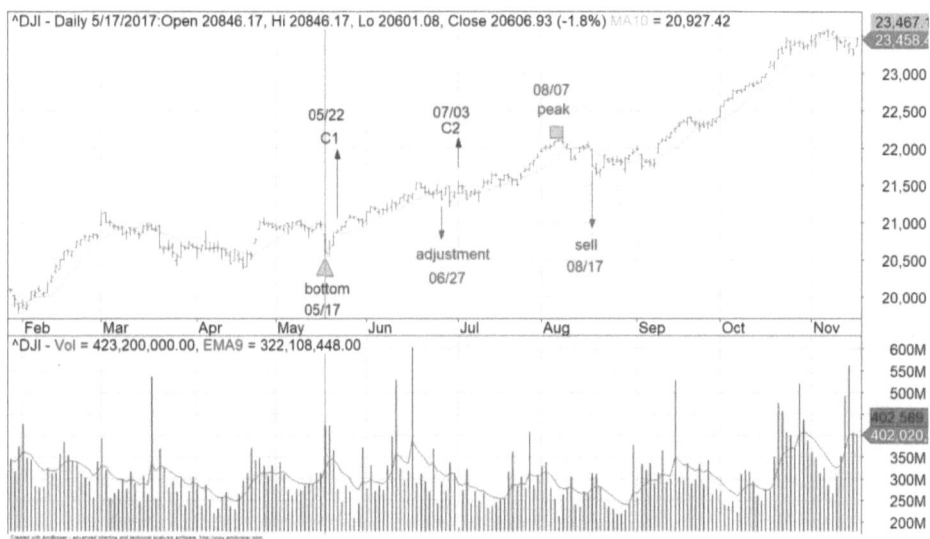

Figure 7-23: Dow Jones (^DJI) daily, 2017, buying and selling confirmation day

We look for an uptrend market confirmation signal:

➤ **05/17/2017: the bottom day.**
➤ **05/22/2017: the confirmation day**, the third day from the bottom day, ^DJI: 20,894.83 > MA10 (20,886.62), rose by 1.4% vs. the bottom day, that is an up-channel signal. From that day, we can consider buying stocks.
➤ **06/27/2017: big adjustment**, even we have to consider to sell stocks.
➤ **07/03/2017: confirmation again.**
➤ **Market uptrend until 08/17/2017**: under MA10, break up-channel. We should sell all the stock on that day.

b. *Analyze stocks, buy and sell*

➢ From the confirmation day to the day before "sell-out" day, every day we explore and control the stock whose R.S > R.S of the general market (^DJI, ^GSPC, ^IXIC), and I.S >= 85%. We rank I.S and R.S from high to low. **This list is called the "Best leading stocks" list of the day.**

➢ From this list, we make a list shorter with breakout condition, ">MA10" condition, and draw the one-year mindset price of the current base.

➢ Check the criteria for buying point.

➢ Check fundamental analysis conditions.

➢ Sort and rank by section and industry.

✦ **On 05/22/2017, we have the list:**

- R.S of general market on 05/22/2017 = Max R.S (^DJI, ^GSPC, ^IXIC) = 2.0% (of ^IXIC).

- Use Microsoft Excel or Explore Tool of Amibroker; we can have the "Best leading stocks" list of 05/22/2017.

- We make it shorter with breakout condition, and ">MA10" condition.

Analysis1   ⏷ ✕

🔲 Scan 👓 Explore ▾ ✅ Backtest ▾ ☆ Optimize ▾ | ▥ ▾ ▢ ▾ ✂ ▾ ▥ |

Formula C:\Users\MSi\Desktop\USA-filter 2.afl   ▾ 📂 📖 |

Apply to *All symbols ▾ ▼ | Range From-To dates ▾ | 5/22/2017 ▥▾ | 5/22/2017 ▥▾ |

Ticker	Date/Time	C	B.O	1	>Ma10...	I.S...	2	R.S	3	%Date-BottomMarket	%Date-Confirmation	Pivot
PTE	5/22/2017	16.78	B.O		1		1.00	46.9		47.5	0.0	1
CALA	5/22/2017	16.50	B.O		1		1.00	26.9		51.4	0.0	1
SOHU	5/22/2017	49.22	B.O		1		1.00	18.5		25.2	0.0	1
AAOI	5/22/2017	71.24	B.O		1		1.00	16.1		52.2	0.0	1
CYOU	5/22/2017	40.18	B.O		1		1.00	15.3		29.3	0.0	1
ICHR	5/22/2017	22.39	B.O		1		1.00	13.4		18.3	0.0	1
MTSI	5/22/2017	60.84	B.O		1		1.00	12.7		36.0	0.0	1
SPKE	5/22/2017	20.50	B.O		1		1.00	11.3		30.2	0.0	1
LITE	5/22/2017	57.35	B.O		1		1.00	10.2		22.0	0.0	1
NVMI	5/22/2017	26.04	B.O		1		1.00	9.5		36.3	0.0	1
BF-B	5/22/2017	45.54	B.O		1		1.00	8.9		17.6	0.0	1
BX	5/22/2017	31.88	B.O		1		1.00	8.7		8.9	0.0	1
AXGN	5/22/2017	15.25	B.O		1		1.00	8.5		29.8	0.0	1
VEEV	5/22/2017	62.07	B.O		1		1.00	8.2		14.6	0.0	1
BAH	5/22/2017	38.50	B.O		1		1.00	8.1		8.2	0.0	1
RAVN	5/22/2017	32.75	B.O		1		1.00	7.9		7.9	0.0	1
BF-A	5/22/2017	34.35	B.O		1		1.00	7.7		17.6	0.0	1
FRPT	5/22/2017	14.75	B.O		1		1.00	7.7		21.9	0.0	1
SGMS	5/22/2017	24.00	B.O		1		1.00	7.4		7.4	0.0	1
PI	5/22/2017	44.38	B.O		1		1.00	7.2		17.3	0.0	1
SQ	5/22/2017	20.95	B.O		1		1.00	7.1		7.1	0.0	1
YUMC	5/22/2017	36.91	B.O		1		1.00	6.6		9.3	0.0	1
HLT	5/22/2017	65.25	B.O		1		1.00	6.4		7.9	0.0	1
ZBRA	5/22/2017	103...	B.O		1		1.00	5.7		10.0	0.0	1
DK	5/22/2017	26.04	B.O		1		1.00	5.6		10.4	0.0	1
DTEGY	5/22/2017	20.22	B.O		1		1.00	5.3		12.0	0.0	1
UPLD	5/22/2017	22.97	B.O		1		1.00	5.3		11.7	0.0	1
IMOS	5/22/2017	19.20	B.O		1		1.00	5.0		10.0	0.0	1
ISRG	5/22/2017	297...	B.O		1		1.00	4.8		6.1	0.0	1
TILE	5/22/2017	20.15	B.O		1		1.00	4.7		5.5	0.0	1
JKHY	5/22/2017	102...	B.O		1		1.00	4.4		6.4	0.0	1
XLNX	5/22/2017	67.52	B.O		1		1.00	4.3		7.3	0.0	1
WIFI	5/22/2017	16.00	B.O		1		1.00	4.2		17.9	0.0	1
KWEB	5/22/2017	49.98	B.O		1		1.00	4.1		11.5	0.0	1
PGJ	5/22/2017	39.66	B.O		1		1.00	4.1		11.2	0.0	1
EWO	5/22/2017	21.38	B.O		1		1.00	4.0		7.3	0.0	1
DELL	5/22/2017	37.31	B.O		1		1.00	3.8		4.2	0.0	1
SYK	5/22/2017	138...	B.O		1		1.00	3.8		3.8	0.0	1
HBMD	5/22/2017	19.10	B.O		1		1.00	3.8		4.1	0.0	1
AEE	5/22/2017	56.42	B.O		1		1.00	3.7		4.1	0.0	1
CDNS	5/22/2017	33.53	B.O		1		1.00	3.5		3.7	0.0	1
LUV	5/22/2017	58.92	B.O		1		1.00	3.3		3.3	0.0	1
TOL	5/22/2017	38.03	B.O		1		1.00	3.2		4.3	0.0	1
VMW	5/22/2017	95.24	B.O		1		1.00	3.2		3.2	0.0	1

|◀ ◀ ▶ ▶| **Result list** / Info \ Walk Forward /

Figure 7-24: Table, list stocks on 05/22/2017 that Breakout, R.S of stocks is higher than R.S of the indexes, the price is higher than MA10

(the actual list is longer than the above-displayed table)

From the above stock list, draw a one-year mindset price for all stocks, check "buy" criteria. Some picture as follows:

1. PolarityTE, Inc. (PTE):

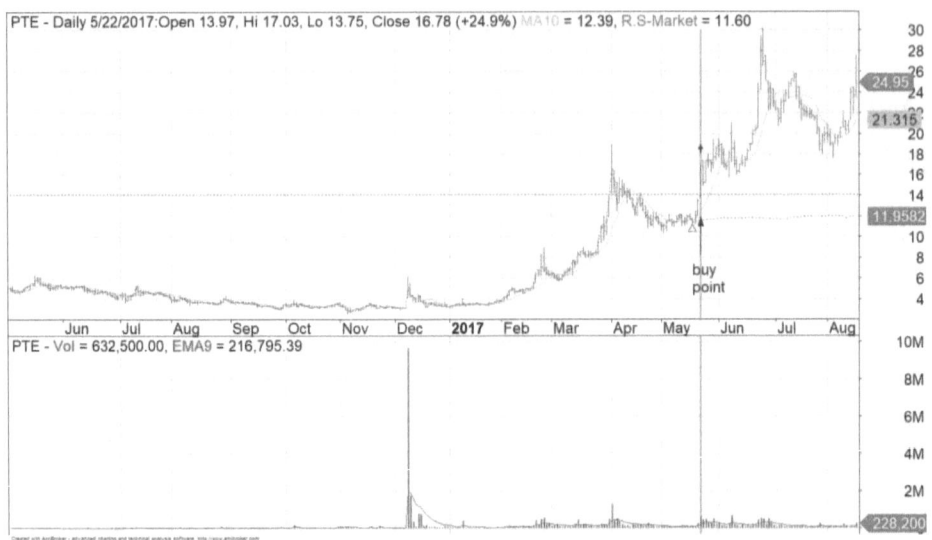

Figure 7-25: (PTE) daily, 2017, buying point

- ➢ Good runner, 05/22/2017 is the buying day.
- ➢ Able to take profit at 20%.
- ➢ Stock's R.S is always greater than R.S of the general market.
- ➢ No emergency sell signal.

2. Calithera Biosciences, Inc. (CALA):

Figure 7-26: (CALA) daily, 2017, buying point

➢ Good runner, but 05/22/2017 is NOT buying day; the price on 05/22/2017 quite high, not good to buy.
➢ Able to take profit at 20%.
➢ Stock's R.S is always greater than R.S of the general market.
➢ No emergency sell signal.

3. Sohu.com Limited (SOHU):

Figure 7-27: (SOHU) daily, 2017, buying point

- ➢ Good runner, but 05/22/2017 is NOT buying day; the price on 05/22/2017 quite high, not good to buy.
- ➢ Able to take profit at 20%.
- ➢ Stock's R.S is always higher than R.S of the general market.
- ➢ No emergency sell signal.

Do similarly for the rest of the stocks in the above table.

- ✦ For all the days in the period from February 5, 2017, to August 8, 2017, we do as same as above. We can add new stocks into the list of daily "Best leading stocks" or eliminate the ones that have not complied.
- ✦ In the list, we check the breakout stocks daily, drawing the one-year mindset price line for the unpainted stocks in the previous days. Do not forget to check the fundamental analysis conditions. Find out the stocks containing the good buying points on that day as per the principle.

✦ If we are holding some stocks, it is necessary to daily check whether these stocks meet the conditions of "good runner," belong to the "Best leading stocks" list, and not violate the principle of emergency selling. If these stocks do not comply with these criteria, we should not hold stocks anymore.

c. *List of stocks having buying points in the period from 05/23/2017 to 08/16/2017 is very successful:*

OPNT_Opiant Pharmaceuticals, Inc., MYOK_MyoKardia, Inc., DVAX_Dynavax Technologies Corporation, BGNE_BeiGene, Ltd., STMP_Stamps.com Inc., SPEX_Spherix Incorporated, YRD_Yirendai Ltd., HIIQ_Health Insurance Innovations, Inc., CO_Global Cord Blood Corporation, NVCR_NovoCure Limited, CUTR_Cutera, Inc., NRG_NRG Energy, Inc., BZUN_Baozun Inc., KEM_Kemet Corporation, FGEN_FibroGen, Inc, ARNA_Arena Pharmaceuticals, Inc., PBYI_Puma Biotechnology Inc, PTE_PolarityTE, Inc., ATHM_Autohome Inc., ACH_Aluminum Corporation of China Limited, YELP_Yelp Inc., FOLD_Amicus Therapeutics, Inc., GTS_Triple-S Management Corporation, SEDG_SolarEdge Technologies, Inc., HTHT_Huazhu Group Limited, SYX_Systemax Inc., APPF_AppFolio, Inc., SGMS_Scientific Games Corp, LGIH_LGI Homes, Inc., CAI_CAI International, Inc., TRHC_Tabula Rasa HealthCare, Inc., OTIC_Otonomy, Inc., OMER_Omeros Corporation, TREE_LendingTree, Inc., TCMD_Tactile Systems Technology, Inc., JOUT_Johnson Outdoors Inc., TGH_Textainer Group Holdings Limited, ONCE_Spark Therapeutics, Inc., CAR_Avis Budget Group, Inc., RTRX_Retrophin, Inc., EXEL_Exelixis, Inc., PTLA_Portola Pharmaceuticals, Inc., EVI_EVI Industries, Inc., INAP_Internap Corporation, MTW_Manitowoc Company, Inc. (The), JKS_JinkoSolar Holding Company Limited, MCRB_Seres Therapeutics, Inc., CVNA_Carvana Co., OSUR_OraSure Technologies, Inc., XLRN_Acceleron Pharma Inc., TAL_TAL Education Group, CMTL_Comtech Telecommunications Corp., UBNT_Ubiquiti Networks, Inc., AERI_Aerie Pharmaceuticals, Inc., ESPR_Esperion Therapeutics, Inc., GDEN_Golden Entertainment, Inc., HCC_Warrior Met Coal, Inc., MRAM_Everspin Technologies, Inc., QDEL_Quidel Corporation, ALRM_Alarm.com Holdings, Inc., TTWO_Take-Two Interactive Software, Inc., MYGN_Myriad Genetics, Inc., YY_YY Inc., XENT_Intersect ENT, Inc., BABA_Alibaba Group Holding Limited, TRUP_Trupanion, Inc., FSLR_First Solar, Inc., LPSN_LivePerson, Inc., SCHN_Schnitzer Steel Industries, Inc., PTCT_PTC Therapeutics, Inc., GDOT_Green Dot Corporation, VEDL_Vedanta Limited, MED_MEDIFAST INC, PETS_PetMed Express, Inc., SPR_Spirit Aerosystems Holdings, Inc., GSM_Ferroglobe PLC, RACE_Ferrari N.V., OSTK_Overstock.com, Inc., JOBS_51job, Inc., PODD_Insulet Corporation, WGO_Winnebago Industries, Inc., BLRX_BioLineRx Ltd., BA_Boeing Company (The), CLVS_Clovis Oncology, Inc., DBVT_DBV Technologies S.A., SUPN_Supernus Pharmaceuticals, Inc., AJRD_Aerojet Rocketdyne Holdings, Inc. , TPL_Texas Pacific Land Trust, BEAT_BioTelemetry, Inc., CSIQ_Canadian Solar Inc., CMCO_Columbus McKinnon Corporation, KMPR_Kemper Corporation, TEO_Telecom Argentina Stet - France Telecom S.A., NRC_National Research Corporation, BSET_Bassett Furniture Industries, Incorporated, IRTC_iRhythm Technologies, Inc., FIZZ_National Beverage Corp., TBK_Triumph Bancorp, Inc., VRTU_Virtusa Corporation, CVTI_Covenant Transportation Group, Inc., VRTX_Vertex Pharmaceuticals Incorporated, AAWW_Atlas Air

Worldwide Holdings, AAN_Aaron's, Inc., QUOT_Quotient Technology Inc., BCO_Brink's Company (The), CHTR_Charter Communications, Inc., MOD_Modine Manufacturing Company, TPIC_TPI Composites, Inc., GRUB_GrubHub Inc., PNTR_Pointer Telocation Ltd., ENTA_Enanta Pharmaceuticals, Inc., SLP_Simulations Plus, Inc., ENV_Envestnet, Inc, IHC_Independence Holding Company, TSU_TIM Participacoes S.A., ATEX_pdvWireless, Inc., LILAK_Liberty Latin America Ltd., SYRS_Syros Pharmaceuticals, Inc., HCM_Hutchison China MediTech Limited, GPX_GP Strategies Corporation, AABA_Altaba Inc., CORT_Corcept Therapeutics Incorporated, ALGN_Align Technology, Inc., WUBA_58.com Inc., BHVN_Biohaven Pharmaceutical Holding Company Ltd., HOME_At Home Group Inc., AVA_Avista Corporation, LILA_Liberty Latin America Ltd., SQM_Sociedad Quimica y Minera S.A., TLND_Talend S.A., CWST_Casella Waste Systems, Inc., SP_SP Plus Corporation, PSTG_Pure Storage, Inc. , SAGE_Sage Therapeutics, Inc., VVI_Viad Corp, LBRDA_Liberty Broadband Corporation, FOR_Forestar Group Inc, BSAC_Banco Santander Chile, WIFI_Boingo Wireless, Inc., IPGP_IPG Photonics Corporation, CHGG_Chegg, Inc., NVTR_Nuvectra Corporation, CBB_Cincinnati Bell Inc,. SAFM_Sanderson Farms, Inc., EBS_Emergent Biosolutions, Inc., MMSI_Merit Medical Systems, Inc., SERV_ServiceMaster Global Holdings, Inc., THG_The Hanover Insurance Group, Inc., CWH_Camping World Holdings, Inc., BTU_Peabody Energy Corporation, FCX_Freeport-McMoran, Inc., TECK_Teck Resources Ltd, PVH_PVH Corp., SEM_Select Medical Holdings Corporation, SAIA_Saia, Inc., APTS_Preferred Apartment Communities, Inc., ANET_Arista Networks, Inc., KAI_Kadant Inc, LBRDK_Liberty Broadband Corporation, VFC_V.F. Corporation, LAND_Gladstone Land Corporation, OMCL_Omnicell, Inc., RP_RealPage, Inc., TRK_Speedway Motorsports, Inc., PYPL_PayPal Holdings, Inc., NVEE_NV5 Global, Inc., AVAV_AeroVironment, Inc., CG_The Carlyle Group L.P., HURC_Hurco Companies, Inc., ETSY_Etsy, Inc., SKX_Skechers U.S.A., Inc., SGC_Superior Group of Companies, Inc., SUPV_Grupo Supervielle S.A., TSBK_Timberland Bancorp, Inc., BLUE_bluebird bio, Inc., MEDP_Medpace Holdings, Inc., LAKE_Lakeland Industries, Inc., EXAS_Exact Sciences Corporation, SRG_Seritage Growth Properties, ICLR_ICON plc, IBP_Installed Building Products, Inc., CPRI_Capri Holdings Limited, ALLY_Ally Financial Inc., INST_Instructure, Inc., AYX_Alteryx, Inc., PRIM_Primoris Services Corporation, SQ_Square, Inc., TRTN_Triton International Limited, HRB_H&R Block, Inc., AVNS_Avanos Medical, Inc., AX_Axos Financial, Inc., CNA_CNA Financial Corporation, KSU_Kansas City Southern, CONN_Conn's, Inc., GLIBA_GCI Liberty, Inc., TPRE_Third Point Reinsurance Ltd., GLG_Bat Group, Inc., ALXN_Alexion Pharmaceuticals, Inc., WERN_Werner Enterprises, Inc., CACC_Credit Acceptance Corporation, KALU_Kaiser Aluminum Corporation, NVDA_NVIDIA Corporation, BBY_Best Buy Co., Inc., MRCY_Mercury Systems Inc, NWPX_Northwest Pipe Company, NEP_NextEra Energy Partners, LP, EPAY_Bottomline Technologies, Inc., MPX_Marine Products Corporation, PLOW_Douglas Dynamics, Inc., LPLA_LPL Financial Holdings Inc., INBK_First Internet Bancorp, RICK_RCI Hospitality Holdings, Inc., LORL_Loral Space and Communications, Inc., RYAAY_Ryanair Holdings plc, LMAT_LeMaitre Vascular, Inc., MTOR_Meritor, Inc., BREW_Craft Brew Alliance, Inc., WF_Woori Bank, BIDU_Baidu, Inc., ETFC_E*TRADE Financial Corporation, MFC_Manulife Financial Corp, TREX_Trex Company, Inc., COT_Cott Corporation, RVNC_Revance Therapeutics, Inc., PLNT_Planet Fitness, Inc., OMF_OneMain Holdings, Inc., LYV_Live Nation Entertainment, Inc., STN_Stantec Inc, WBC_Wabco Holdings Inc., TNET_TriNet Group, Inc., DAN_Dana Incorporated, NAV_Navistar International Corporation, AMTD_TD Ameritrade Holding Corporation, AA_Alcoa Corporation, LL_Lumber Liquidators Holdings, Inc, ATI_Allegheny Technologies

Incorporated, GLOG_GasLog LP., HAIN_The Hain Celestial Group, Inc., FOXF_Fox Factory Holding Corp., SNDR_Schneider National, Inc., BMI_Badger Meter, Inc.,

Some charts of the successful stocks:

OPNT

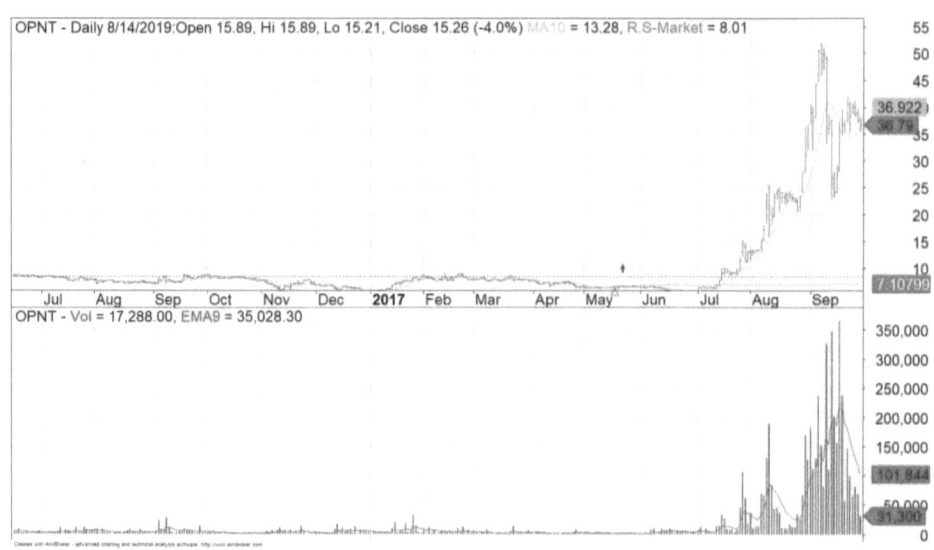

MYOK

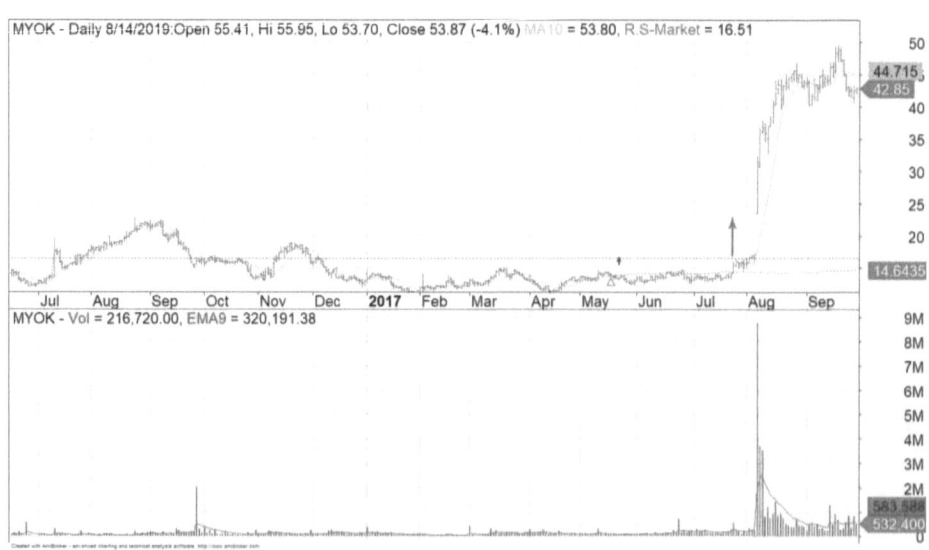

BGNE

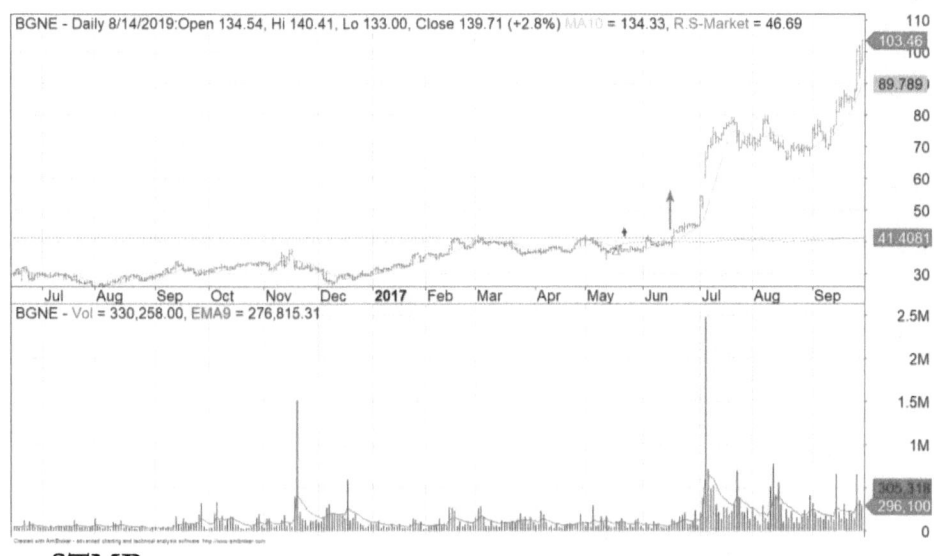

STMP

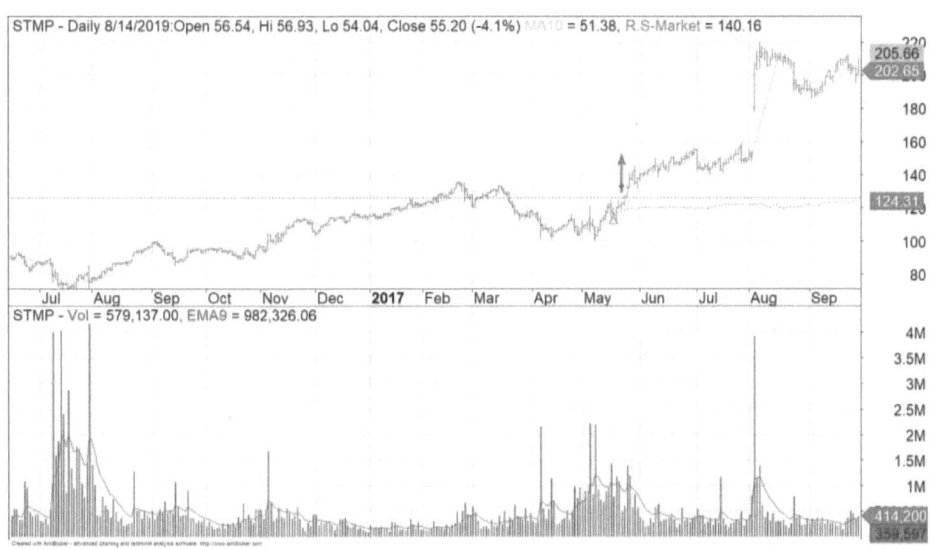

YRD

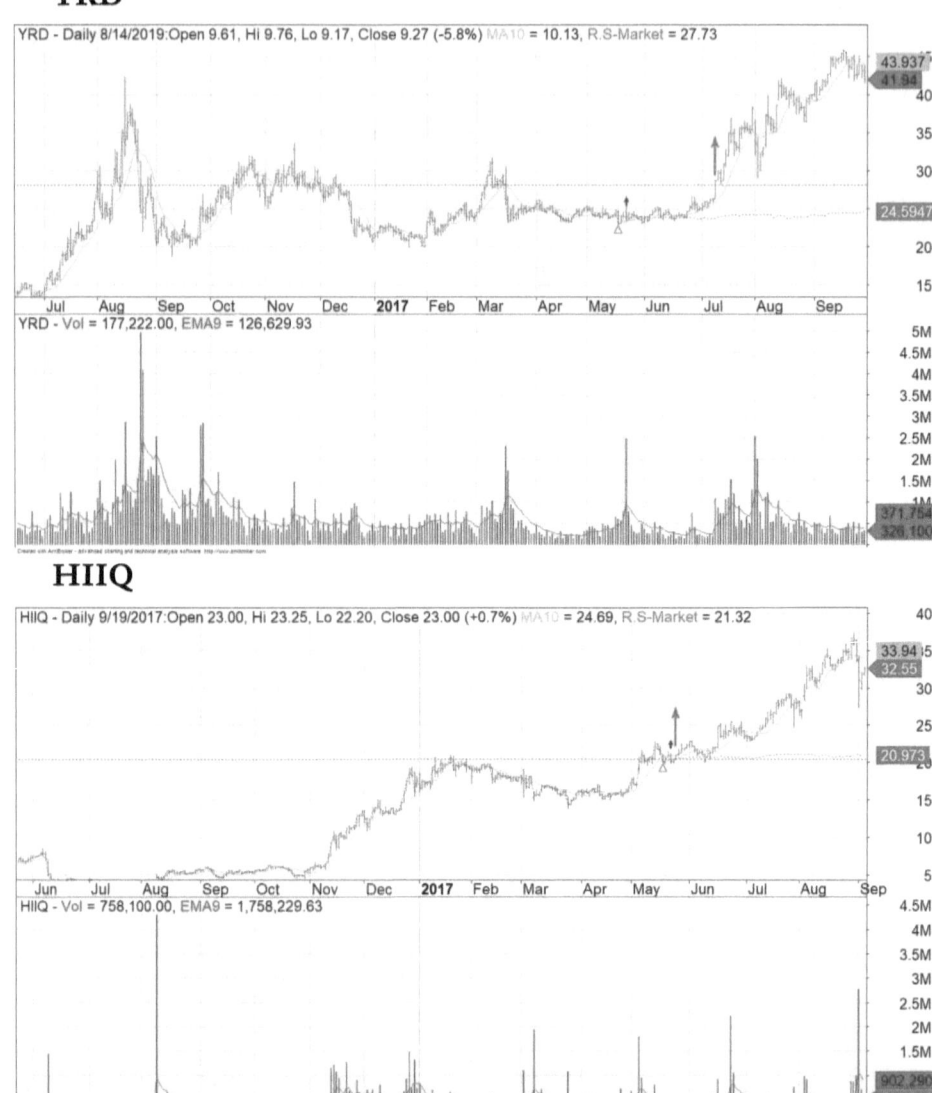

HIIQ

Figure 7-28: Some charts of the successful stocks

II. Uptrend period from 05/31/2019 to 07/15/2019:

a. Check the general market

Figure 7-29: Dow Jones (^DJI) daily, 2019, buying/ selling confirmation day

We look for an uptrend market confirmation signal:

❖ **05/31/2019: the bottom day.**
❖ **06/05/2019: the confirmation day**, the third day since the bottom day, ^DJI: 25,539.57 > MA10 (25,300.34), rose by 2.9% vs. the bottom day, up-channel signal. From that day, we can consider buying stocks.
❖ **Market uptrend until 07/25/2019**: under MA10, break up-channel. We should sell all the stock on that day.

b. Analyze stocks, buy and sell

❖ From the confirmation day to the day before "sell-out" day, every day we find the "Best leading stocks" list.

Shin Nakamoto

❖ From this list, we make a shortlist by breakout condition, ">=MA10" condition, and draw the one-year mindset price of the current base.
❖ Check the criteria for buying point.
❖ Check fundamental conditions.
❖ Sort and rank by section and industry.

⬇ **On 06/05/2019, we find the stocks having buy point as follows:**
- R.S of general market on 06/05/2019 = Max R.S (^DJI, ^GSPC, ^IXIC) = 2.9% (of ^DJI).
- We get the "Best leading stocks" list, and shorten by breakout condition, and ">=MA10" condition.

Analysis1

Scan Explore Backtest ▾ Optimize ▾

Formula C:\Users\MSi\Desktop\USA-filter 2.afl

Apply to *All symbols Range From-To dates 6/ 5/2019 6/ 5/2019

Ticker	Date/Time	C	B.O	⚡1	>Ma10	I.S	⚡2	R.S	⚡3	%Date-BottomMarket	%Date-Confirmation	Pivot
TTD	6/5/2019	232.30	B.O		1		1.00	16.8		19.0	0.0	1
NSSC	6/5/2019	30.34	B.O		1		1.00	13.5		15.6	0.0	1
MSON	6/5/2019	25.32	B.O		1		1.00	13.1		30.4	0.0	1
UAA	6/5/2019	25.76	B.O		1		1.00	13.0		13.0	0.0	1
ROKU	6/5/2019	101.71	B.O		1		1.00	12.5		22.1	0.0	1
BOOM	6/5/2019	75.76	B.O		1		1.00	12.0		14.5	0.0	1
ROAD	6/5/2019	14.46	B.O		1		1.00	11.1		11.1	0.0	1
WING	6/5/2019	88.27	B.O		1		1.00	10.8		13.1	0.0	1
QTRX	6/5/2019	28.32	B.O		1		1.00	10.6		29.7	0.0	1
CHDN	6/5/2019	109.07	B.O		1		1.00	10.6		14.5	0.0	1
INT	6/5/2019	32.14	B.O		1		1.00	10.3		10.3	0.0	1
TTEK	6/5/2019	74.31	B.O		1		1.00	10.1		13.1	0.0	1
IIPR	6/5/2019	92.01	B.O		1		1.00	9.5		12.6	0.0	1
RGEN	6/5/2019	75.73	B.O		1		1.00	9.0		13.0	0.0	1
ARNA	6/5/2019	57.29	B.O		1		1.00	8.1		8.1	0.0	1
ZTS	6/5/2019	108.50	B.O		1		1.00	7.4		7.4	0.0	1
AZPN	6/5/2019	121.67	B.O		1		1.00	7.1		9.5	0.0	1
OSIS	6/5/2019	110.85	B.O		1		1.00	7.0		9.2	0.0	1
LIN	6/5/2019	192.75	B.O		1		1.00	6.8		6.8	0.0	1
MSCI	6/5/2019	234.50	B.O		1		1.00	6.6		8.4	0.0	1
ATRO	6/5/2019	43.37	B.O		1		1.00	6.6		6.6	0.0	1
SHOP	6/5/2019	292.52	B.O		1		1.00	6.4		10.4	0.0	1
PGR	6/5/2019	83.34	B.O		1		1.00	5.1		7.2	0.0	1
BLL	6/5/2019	64.45	B.O		1		1.00	5.0		6.5	0.0	1
ECL	6/5/2019	193.12	B.O		1		1.00	4.9		6.7	0.0	1
FE	6/5/2019	43.07	B.O		1		1.00	4.4		5.2	0.0	1
PPA	6/5/2019	63.35	B.O		1		1.00	4.3		4.3	0.0	1
PNW	6/5/2019	97.79	B.O		1		1.00	4.1		5.2	0.0	1
STAG	6/5/2019	30.37	B.O		1		1.00	4.1		4.4	0.0	1
CSGP	6/5/2019	530.13	B.O		1		1.00	4.0		6.1	0.0	1
CHE	6/5/2019	340.18	B.O		1		1.00	3.7		3.7	0.0	1
MMS	6/5/2019	73.88	B.O		1		1.00	3.7		5.5	0.0	1
IEX	6/5/2019	158.11	B.O		1		1.00	3.5		5.0	0.0	1
KO	6/5/2019	50.78	B.O		1		1.00	3.4		4.5	0.0	1
ATR	6/5/2019	117.13	B.O		1		1.00	3.4		3.9	0.0	1
CINF	6/5/2019	101.60	B.O		1		1.00	3.4		4.0	0.0	1
IDU	6/5/2019	152.06	B.O		1		1.00	3.3		3.9	0.0	1
ETR	6/5/2019	100.24	B.O		1		1.00	3.3		4.8	0.0	1
BUI	6/5/2019	21.76	B.O		1		1.00	3.2		3.2	0.0	1
XLU	6/5/2019	60.14	B.O		1		1.00	3.2		3.7	0.0	1
VRSK	6/5/2019	144.35	B.O		1		1.00	3.1		3.4	0.0	1
PSA	6/5/2019	244.89	B.O		1		1.00	2.9		6.4	0.0	1
PSA-...	6/5/2019	25.20	B.O		1		1.00	1.1		1.7	0.0	1

Info Walk Forward **Result list**

Figure 7-30: Table, list stocks on 06/05/2019, breakout, R.S of stocks is higher than R.S of the indexes, the price is higher than MA10

(the actual list is longer than the above-displayed table)

Draw a one-year mindset price for all stocks, check "buy" criteria. Some picture as follows:

1. The Trade Desk, Inc. (TTD):

Figure 7-31: (TTD) daily, Aug.2019, buying point

➢ Good runner, buying point is on 06/04/2019 – one day sooner than the confirmation day.
➢ Able to take profit at 20%.
➢ Stock's R.S is always greater than R.S of the general market.
➢ No emergency sell signal.

2. Napco Security Technologies, Inc. (NSSC):

Figure 7-32: (NSSC) daily, Aug.2019, buying point

- ➢ Not good runner, buy point on 06/05/2019.
- ➢ Sell stock on 6/25/2019, because of R.S of the stock is less than R.S of the general market.
- ➢ Liquidation, at a profit of 7.1%.
- ➢ No emergency sell signal.

3. Misonix, Inc. (MSON):

Figure 7-33: (MSON) daily, Aug.2019, buying point

> ➢ Good runner, but 06/05/2019 is NOT buying day; the price on 06/05/2019 quite high, not good to buy.
> ➢ Able to take profit at 20% from an excellent buy point.
> ➢ Stock's R.S is always higher than R.S of the general market.
> ➢ No emergency sell signal.

Do similarly for the rest of the stocks in the above table.

➕ For all days in the period from 06/05/2019 to 07/24/2019, we do the same, including: updating the list of "Best leading stocks," drawing the one-year mindset price line, finding stocks containing buying points on the day, reviewing fundamental analysis, checking portfolios.

c. *The list of stocks having buying points in the period from 06/05/2019 to 07/25/2019 is very successful:*

IIPR_Innovative Industrial Properties, Inc., EHTH_eHealth, Inc., CRVL_CorVel Corp., ZYME_Zymeworks Inc., PAGS_PagSeguro Digital Ltd., COUP_Coupa Software Incorporated,

KL_Kirkland Lake Gold Ltd., RGEN_Repligen Corporation, QIWI_QIWI plc, CIEN_Ciena Corporation, EVBG_Everbridge, Inc., PLAN_Anaplan, Inc., CTLT_Catalent, Inc., ZM_Zoom Video Communications, Inc., HALL_Hallmark Financial Services, Inc., SLP_Simulations Plus, Inc., PRVB_Provention Bio, Inc., GLOB_Globant S.A., TTEC_TTEC Holdings, Inc., MANH_Manhattan Associates, Inc., AXNX_Axonics Modulation Technologies, Inc., CSII_Cardiovascular Systems, Inc., PSN_Parsons Corporation, RPD_Rapid7, Inc., NRC_National Research Corporation, KRYS_Krystal Biotech, Inc., IIIV_i3 Verticals, Inc., HYGS_Hydrogenics Corporation, PAYS_Paysign, Inc., INSP_Inspire Medical Systems, Inc., KOD_Kodiak Sciences Inc, EIDX_Eidos Therapeutics, Inc., ADVM_Adverum Biotechnologies, Inc., LOOP_Loop Industries, Inc., CLCT_Collectors Universe, Inc., FCN_FTI Consulting, Inc., LK_Luckin Coffee Inc., TDY_Teledyne Technologies Incorporated, SMPL_The Simply Good Foods Company, MTH_Meritage Corporation, AVLR_Avalara, Inc., SSFN_Stewardship Financial Corp, DBD_Diebold Nixdorf Incorporated, NVCR_NovoCure Limited, ENPH_Enphase Energy, Inc., RING_iShares MSCI Global Gold Miners ETF, IOVA_Iovance Biotherapeutics, Inc., SNAP_Snap Inc., SMAR_Smartsheet Inc., CASY_Caseys General Stores, Inc., RFL_Rafael Holdings, Inc., GSHD_Goosehead Insurance, Inc., AXSM_Axsome Therapeutics, Inc., GNRC_Generac Holdlings Inc., GLPG_Galapagos NV, ARGX_argenx SE, MGTX_MeiraGTx Holdings plc, PTGX_Protagonist Therapeutics, Inc., ODT_Odonate Therapeutics, Inc., BX_The Blackstone Group Inc., BPMC_Blueprint Medicines Corporation, RGLD_Royal Gold, Inc., VIAV_Viavi Solutions Inc., SAM_Boston Beer Company, Inc. (The), HFFG_HF Foods Group Inc., CSOD_Cornerstone OnDemand, Inc., MLHR_Herman Miller, Inc., SAH_Sonic Automotive, Inc., UGLD_Credit Suisse AG, AZUL_Azul S.A., RUN_Sunrun Inc., SE_Sea Limited, SHAK_Shake Shack, Inc., AUDC_AudioCodes Ltd., ARVN_Arvinas, Inc., ESTC_Elastic N.V., LSCC_Lattice Semiconductor Corporation, VCYT_Veracyte, Inc., AU_AngloGold Ashanti Limited, AYX_Alteryx, Inc., OSW_OneSpaWorld Holdings Limited, OFG_OFG Bancorp, WPM_Wheaton Precious Metals Corp., SSRM_SSR Mining Inc., EW_Edwards Lifesciences Corporation, KAR_KAR Auction Services, Inc, PEN_Penumbra, Inc., JYNT_The Joint Corp., HHC_Howard Hughes Corporation (The), GOLD_Barrick Gold Corporation, DXCM_DexCom, Inc., TACO_Del Taco Restaurants, Inc., TER_Teradyne, Inc., CDLX_Cardlytics, Inc., ASML_ASML Holding N.V., SPLK_Splunk Inc., PCMI_PCM, Inc., TRU_TransUnion, FOXF_Fox Factory Holding Corp., HAE_Haemonetics Corporation, NSP_Insperity, Inc., OZM_Och-Ziff Capital Management Group LLC, ICHR_Ichor Holdings, IPHI_Inphi Corporation, GOL_Gol Linhas Aereas Inteligentes S.A., APLS_Apellis Pharmaceuticals, Inc., TWST_Twist Bioscience Corporation, TITN_Titan Machinery Inc., OLED_Universal Display Corporation, BOOT_Boot Barn Holdings, Inc., PI_Impinj, Inc., FB_Facebook, Inc., SA_Seabridge Gold, Inc., ZLAB_Zai Lab Limited, KNL_Knoll, Inc., ARD_Ardagh Group S.A., RARX_Ra Pharmaceuticals, Inc., CRTX_Cortexyme, Inc., SOXX_iShares PHLX SOX Semiconductor Sector Index Fund, ANIK_Anika Therapeutics Inc., HWKN_Hawkins, Inc., ADI_Analog Devices, Inc., POWI_Power Integrations, Inc., CG_The Carlyle Group L.P., ENTG_Entegris, Inc., ODFL_Old Dominion Freight Line, Inc., BYND_Beyond Meat, Inc., TSU_TIM Participacoes S.A., KLAC_KLA Corporation , EDU_New Oriental Education & Technology Group, Inc., SKX_Skechers U.S.A., Inc., JBL_Jabil Inc., PRNB_Principia Biopharma Inc., RCKY_Rocky Brands, Inc., WHR_Whirlpool Corporation, VCEL_Vericel Corporation, MCHP_Microchip Technology Incorporated, FTNT_Fortinet, Inc., SYMC_Symantec Corporation, CRUS_Cirrus Logic, Inc., AXTA_Axalta Coating Systems Ltd., CCMP_Cabot Microelectronics Corporation, MPWR_Monolithic Power Systems, Inc., BUD_Anheuser-Busch Inbev SA, IRDM_Iridium Communications Inc, BBY_Best Buy Co., Inc., ACIA_Acacia Communications, Inc.,

Shin Nakamoto

SSYS_Stratasys, Ltd., AMAT_Applied Materials, Inc., UPS_United Parcel Service, Inc., KURA_Kura Oncology, Inc., AMBA_Ambarella, Inc., GEOS_Geospace Technologies Corporation, MXL_MaxLinear, Inc, CTRP_Ctrip.com International, Ltd., ROG_Rogers Corporation, DRNA_Dicerna Pharmaceuticals, Inc., XLNX_Xilinx, Inc., DIOD_Diodes Incorporated, ATNX_Athenex, Inc., GRFS_Grifols, S.A., REVG_REV Group, Inc., HARP_Harpoon Therapeutics, Inc., FSCT_ForeScout Technologies, Inc., SRPT_Sarepta Therapeutics, Inc., CODA_Coda Octopus Group, Inc., SRI_Stoneridge, Inc., UCTT_Ultra Clean Holdings, Inc., PDEX_Pro-Dex, Inc., TDOC_Teladoc Health, Inc., WGO_Winnebago Industries, Inc., GDS_GDS Holdings Limited, SENEA_Seneca Foods Corp., MTLS_Materialise NV, PAAS_Pan American Silver Corp., MOR_MorphoSys AG, FN_Fabrinet, KNX_Knight Transportation, Inc., IART_Integra LifeSciences Holdings Corporation, RTEC_Rudolph Technologies, Inc., TQQQ_ProShares UltraPro QQQ, HTZ_Hertz Global Holdings, Inc, ALEC_Alector, Inc., MKSI_MKS Instruments, Inc., LMAT_LeMaitre Vascular, Inc., TSEM_Tower Semiconductor Ltd., CAR_Avis Budget Group, Inc., NVTA_Invitae Corporation, GPX_GP Strategies Corporation, ELF_e.l.f. Beauty, Inc., CROX_Crocs, Inc., FNKO_Funko, Inc., FTCH_Farfetch Limited, EVER_EverQuote, Inc.

Some charts of the successful stocks:

IIPR

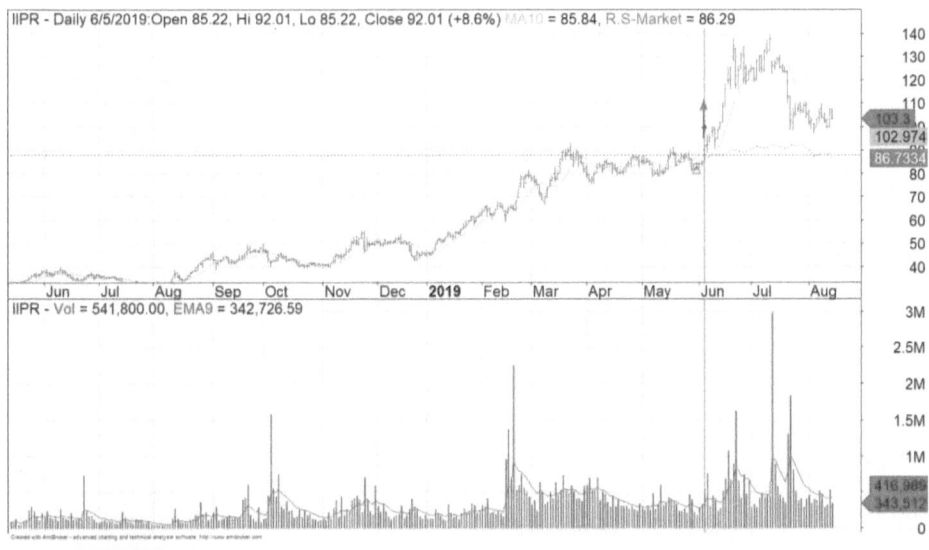

EHTH

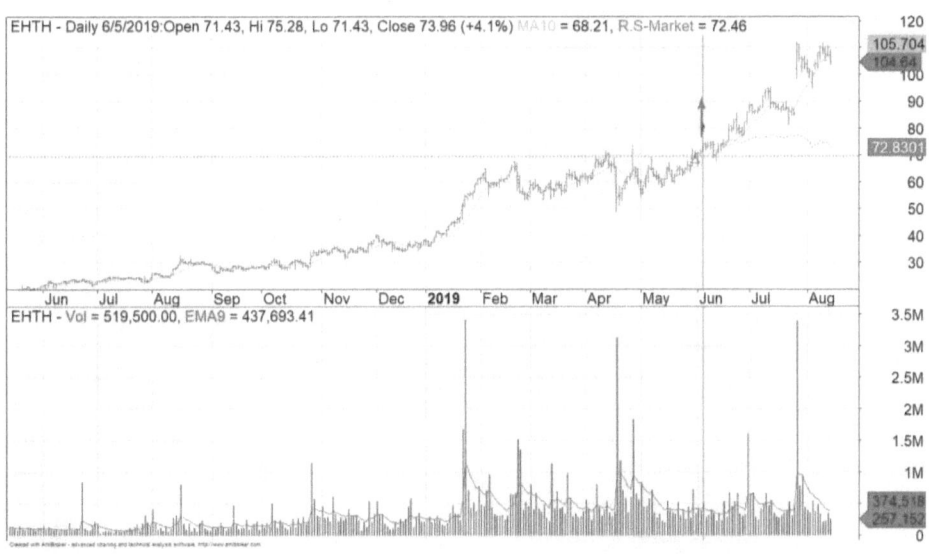

CRVL

PAGS

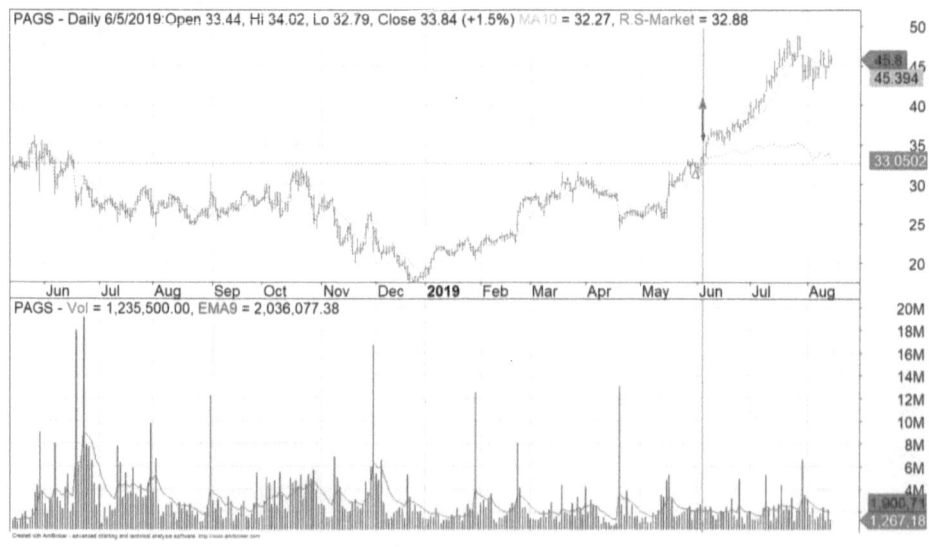

COUP

RGEN

Chapter 8: PORTFOLIO MANAGEMENT

Portfolio management is essential content for both our investing strategies stated in the previous chapters. Managing the portfolio by math, the statistical probability to ensure "optimal" profit and "minimum" risk. We note that profitability is optimal, not maximized, and the most important is risk control.

Why need to manage the portfolio?

❖ Managing the portfolio to manage the increasing disbursement along with the general market movements.

❖ Managing the portfolio to ensure the stock you have chosen is correct, and you have a good position for the next purchase.

❖ Managing the portfolio to optimize profits and minimize risks when holding stocks.

We check out the stocks following the rules of technical analysis and fundamental analysis. However, there is a probability of whether stocks are successful or not.

Buying stocks randomly gives us a chance of 50% winning or failing. By technical analysis and fundamental analysis, we raise the winning rate to 70-85%. In terms of TP = 20%, SL = 7% (TP/SL ratio: 3/1), and a relatively short period, the rate of 50-60% of winning is satisfactory to almost investors. If you can thoroughly apply the method in this book, I firmly believe that you can achieve that.

How to control risks?

According to the analysis above, we estimate a maximum stop-loss of 7% each trade. Take an example, and we can expect profits of $20,000, and accept the risk of $7,000 for the trade of $100,000.

Is this possible to maintain the expected return, but reduce the level of risk? The answer is Yes, we can partially trade, turn the profit of the previous trade into the insurance for the next.

❖ *If you only accept the risk by a half - $ 3,500*, you can buy into 02 lots with the same amount (buying 1 or 2 stocks)
  ➤ The first lot: $50,000, acceptance risk is: 7% x 50,000 = $3,500. After the first lot was bought, you consider deciding whether to buy the second lot or not. If the stock price falls, at the maximum loss of 7%, you will sell stocks. If rising, you wait till getting a profit of 7%, and you start to disburse for the second lot.
  ➤ The second lot: $50,000.

At this point, you bear the maximum risk: $100,000 x 7% - 3,500 (earned profit) = $3,500.

The expected profit still to be at $20,000.

❖ *If you only accept the risk of a quarter - $1,750,* you can buy into 04 lots with the same amount.
  ➤ The first lot: $25,000, acceptance risk is: 7% x 25,000 = $1,750. Wait until getting 7% profit, you continue disbursing for the second lot.
  ➤ The second lot: $25,000, maximum risk if any: 500,000 x 7% - 1,750 (earned profit) = $1,750. If the profit of 2 first lots reaches 7%, you continue disbursing for the 3rd lot.

➤ The 3rd lot: $25,000, maximum risk if any: 750,000 x 7% - 3,500 (earned profit) = $1,750. If the profit of 3 first lots reach 7%, you continue disbursing for the last time.

➤ The 4th lot: Balance $25,000, maximum risk if any: 100,000 x 7% - 5,250 (earned profit) = $1,750.

The expected profit still to be $20,000.

The above is just a typical example; if the profit can reach 5%, we can disburse into the next lot.

How many stocks are reasonable to buy?

To determine how many stocks are appropriate, you consider basing on your capital and risk acceptance. If you hold an enormous amount of money, we should buy many stocks to distribute the risk of loss as well as the risk of liquidation if any. Having a small amount of capital, we should buy a few stocks, but only focusing on 1 - 2 stocks is quite risky.

❖ 1 stock: Put all your eggs in one basket, the highest risk coming from both factors of the general market and the stock itself. If you partially buy into 2 or 3 lots, we can decrease the risk because of insurance, but overall, it is still risky in case of surprising situations.

❖ 2 stocks: Suitable for capital under $30,000. Risk is reduced by half, and the expected profit is still as expected.

❖ 3 - 5 stocks: Suitable for the capital from $30,000 to $1,000,000. You will have the optimal risk management, gain expected profit, and the disbursement schedule is not too long.

❖ More than 5 stocks: only for the big capital, of course, you need to increase the number of stocks. However, how many are appropriate?

Except for the large-cap stocks or blue-chip stocks that can be bought in massive, the investment budget for each other stock should be stopped at a maximum of $150,000 per each stock. Thus, it will be safe on liquidation when taking profit, as well as liquidating in case of unexpected events or abnormal risks.

Many investors are worried that we can fail in management when holding too many stocks. Actually, that is not the problem. Our principle of selling use only technical analysis, complete quantification, no more emotional factors. Even if using some supporting tools, you effortlessly manage the list. Therefore, you manage "selling" properly; managing up to 50 stocks doesn't matter.

However, there is one problem: The period from buying the first lot to full 100% disbursement may last too long because we need "insurance" to go forward. One perfect uptrend without strong shaking, or strong adjusting till "break up-channel day" cannot wait for us to disburse into 8 or 10 lots. Therefore, we consider buying more stocks, but fewer disbursement times (you will buy more than 1 stock per disbursement), so that the buying process is not too slow, causing late lots to encounter a period of reversal market.

In brief, we can buy many stocks per disbursement time, and should not disburse more than 6 times within one short uptrend.

Should we use the margin offered by securities companies?

From the author's point, the answer of yes or no is not important, as long as you can establish your expected profit and acceptable risk. You intend to trade the amount of $300,000, you assume the profit amount and accept the loss amount based on $300,000. However, you withdraw $100,000 for other purposes, you have the capital of $200,000 left but expect the profit and accept the loss unchanged (still at the capital of $300,000). Using the credit of $100,000 doesn't matter, the only difference is the interest you will pay for $100,000.

Chapter 9: MINDMAP OF 2 STRATEGIES

1. STRATEGY 1 – COPY THE LARGEST FUNDS' PORTFOLIOS

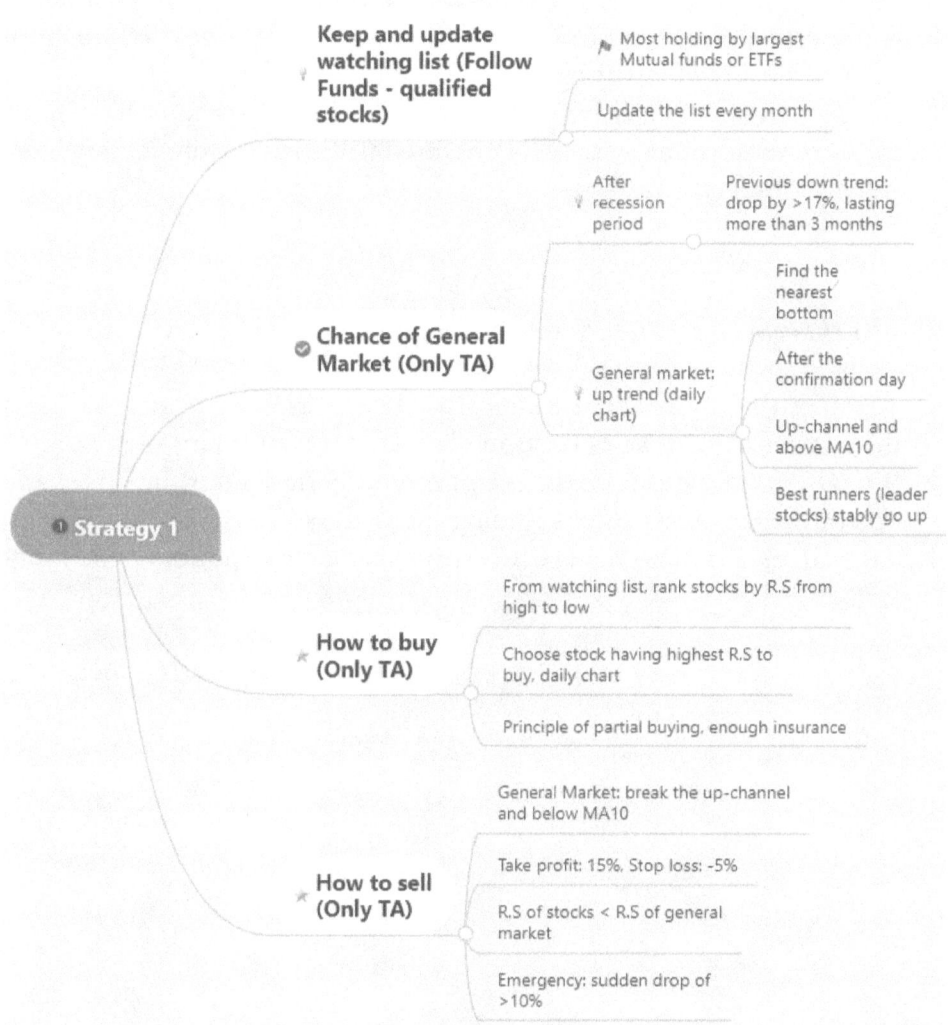

Shin Nakamoto

Why can this method be 100% quantified, eliminate emotions when trading?

❖ Significant investment funds help us to filter the stock list on both sides of quality enterprises and stock liquidity ability.
❖ Assessments and decisions to choose the buying time, selling time, disburse options, the rate of TP, SL are results from technical analysis, basing on specific numbers.

Why is this method effective?

❖ The fact that investment funds have been surviving and growing is the answer to why we choose stocks at the top of their portfolio.
❖ We only follow these funds in an uptrend period, after the crisis, and accept the strongest stocks leading the market.
❖ TP / SL ~ 3/1 ratio helps us to survive and earn money in the long-term.

2. STRATEGY 2 - BUY AND MANAGE THE BEST GROWTH STOCKS

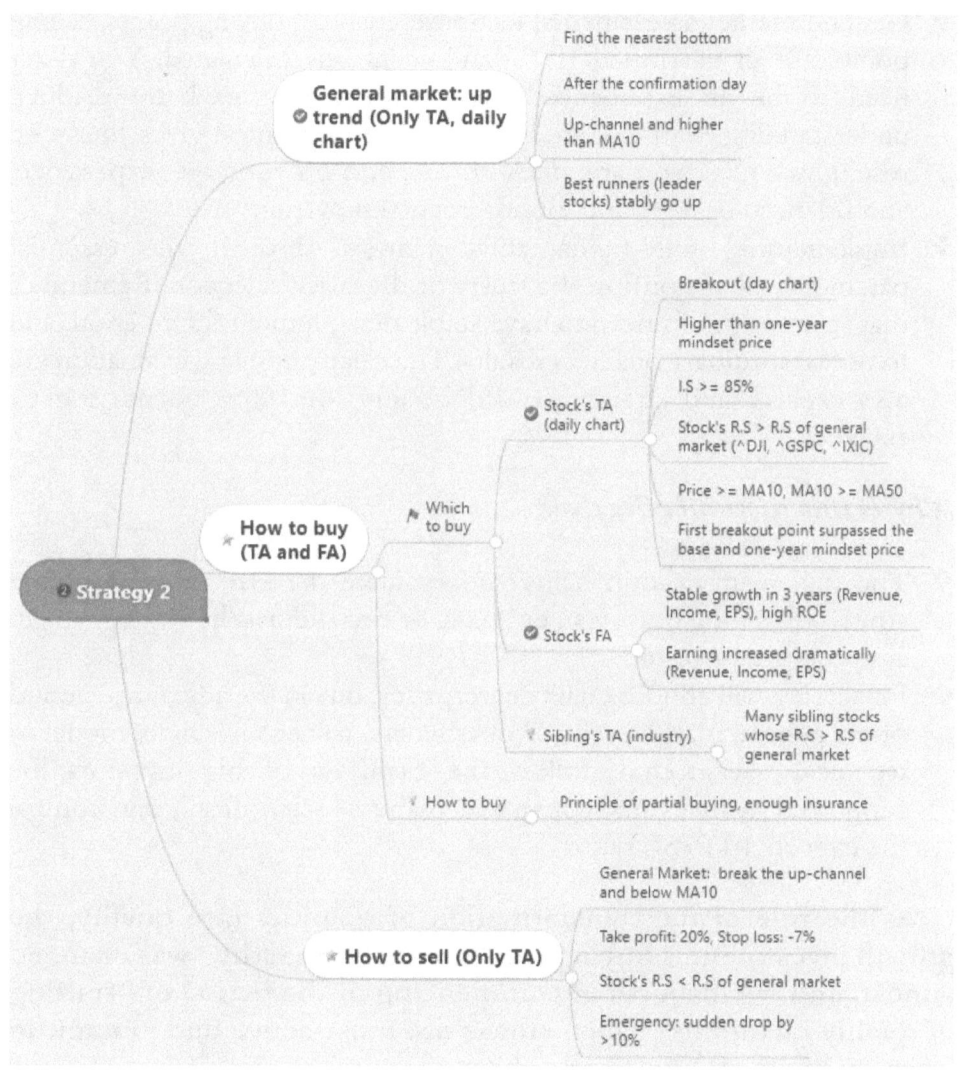

Why does this method completely quantify and eliminate emotions when trading?

❖ General market assessments, technical analysis, buying points, selling points are all quantified 100% and accurately calculated. You don't need to be an experienced investor. All you need are reading, understanding, testing, and applying. The calculation gives the same results, whoever you are, does not depend on your age, experience, and financial background, or arithmetic knowledge.

❖ Implementing the fundamental analysis through the essential parameters shall confirm the trusty of the stock selection. Remember that selected stocks need to have stable development for a period, and have extraordinary business results. The calculation and evaluation are also capable and straightforward because of 100% quantifying by statistics.

Why is this method effective?

❖ The full quantification helps you evaluate the effectiveness of the strategy in a long time, test, evaluate, or even adjust the strategy to get a more optimal result.

❖ Finally, we will choose quality enterprises, buy in the advantage period of the general market, select stocks having a success activity model or technical background, follow the cashflow of big investors, be supported by investors' consensus, disburse scientifically and control the expected TP/SL ratio.

As the rule of the transformation of quantity into quality, the growth investment is buying stocks whose "quantity" was changed almost, and we disburse at commencing of the period of "starting of quality changing," when stocks are most active and vibrant, to jump up to a new higher price base.

FINAL REMARKS

Amidst the vast array of stocks, numerous waves in the market, various layers of information that need to be decoded, I firmly believe that this book is a scientific and practical fulcrum, keep you free from emotions and always be alert when trading.

The author hopes each reader will become an expert on the stock investment, opportunity assessment, risk analysis by using mathematical formulas that the author has simplified to include in this book. Of course, the final goal is that you yourself will create a sustainable income when joining the stock market.

I am very grateful if you can give me one minute and give your review and comment after reading the book. If you have any questions about the content in this book, please send me the email to Shin.nakamoto.jp@gmail.com.

My colleagues and I have been establishing the address: www.bestleadingstocks.com, together with providing the application on the Android and IOS platforms, and it will come out very soon. The aim is to provide market information, the best daily stock list according to the strategy of this book quickly and accurately. If you are busy or want to save time on analyzing, I believe, it will be a place worth visiting regularly.

Thank you.

ABOUT AUTHORS

Shin Nakamoto has a background in mathematics, information technology, and statistical analysis. He has a passion for stock trading and has the ambition to find a formula for winning the stock market. As young, he started by joining some investment funds and operating his private funds very soon. Shin Nakamoto spent many years researching all about successful funds in the world as well as their investment strategies, until now, getting 15 years of experience in both stock and forex trading. Besides, he has completed an MBA course in Tokyo, which made him understand very well of business management and possessing the know-how to accurately business performance.

Shin has very experienced both value investing and growth investing. He understands deeply to nature and core principles each strategy, from approach to process and daily checklist. Shin can use expert level of some technical analysis software like (Amibroker, Metastock, ...), be able to program himself, and build his own tool to scan, filter, explore and rank stock.

In the books on trading guidance, he focuses on two simple strategies: 1. Follow the portfolios of the largest funds, buy in the recovery phase after the recession; 2. Growth investing formula, a strategy already is a packaged process that the beginner can grasp and apply.

With a friendly, non-academic writing style, Shin explains lots of complicated things to easy to understand and enable to do in reality. He will present to readers complete but straightforward information: Approaches, strategies, processes, checklists, examples, and back-test.

Since then, the readers' conviction is unshakable, and account balances will increase significantly and consistently in the future.

Shin finally proves to you that "no secret ingredient," which you heard in the film Kungfu Panda, is not on the screen only.